English - Chinese Bilingual Book
英汉双语

Silly, Silly Mouse
Jamie Book 2

杰米传奇 (第二卷)

鼠目真光 丛书
TRUE LIGHT THROUGH MOUSE EYES

Light of Logos Press

Silly, Silly Mouse
Jamie Book 2
杰米传奇 (第二卷)

Joshua, Sarah
and Yuegang Zhang

Silly, Silly Mouse Jamie Book 2

English and Chinese bilingual text copyright © 2012 by Joshua Zhang, Sarah Zhang and Yuegang Zhang
Illustrations and the photo on the back cover copyright © 2014 by Yuegang Zhang

All rights reserved. Except as permitted under the U. S. copyright Act of 1976, no part of this publication may be reproduced, distributed, or transmitted in any form or by any means, or stored in a database or retrieval system, without the prior written permission of the publisher.

Light of Logos Press
15 Fairfield Rd
Wayland, MA 01778
United States
E. mail: LightOfLogosPress@gmail.com

The English Scripture quotations are from The Holy Bible, English Standard Version® (ESV®), copyright © 2001 by Crossway, a publishing ministry of Good News Publishers. Used by permission. All rights reserved.
中文圣经经文取自和合本。

First English-Simplified Chinese Bilingual Edition: August 2014
First Paperback Edition: August 2014

The characters and events portrayed in this book are fictitious. Any similarity to real persons is coincidental and not intended by the authors.

United State Copyright Office Registration Number and Date:
TXu001791740 / 2012-01-18

Library of Congress Control Number: 2014914196

Publisher's Cataloging-in-Publication Data
Zhang, Joshua Shuen 2004-
 Silly, silly mouse Jamie book 2 / Joshua, Sarah and Yuegang Zhang. – 2nd ed. English Chinese Bilingual ed.
 p. cm.
Summary: Little mouse Jamie thinks he is smart. However, he is very silly. He made lots of trouble and learned hard lessons, but finally became a hero.
 Includes index.
 ISBN 978-0-9896356-2-2 (paperback)

[1. Fantasy Fiction. 2. Mice – Fiction. 3. Christian life – Fiction. 4. Chinese language materials--Bilingual. 5. Christian education--Juvenile fiction.] I. Title.

PZ7.Z4536 Si 2014
[Fic] – dc22

2014914196
10 9 8 7 6 5 4 3 2 1

To the children of all Nations, whom are loved dearly by Jesus Christ!

献给世界各国的小朋友,

耶稣基督深深地爱你们!

Special Thanks to our mom, Meiqin Xie, for her love to make this book possible.

衷心感谢我们的妈妈谢美琴。
她的爱使这本书成为可能。

Gratitude to Pastor Steve Ziyi Chang and his wife Irene, and many other pastors, brothers and sisters for their warm-hearted encouragement and support.

感谢张子义牧师和陈一萍师母、以及很多牧者和兄弟姐妹的热心鼓励和支持。

Thanks to Ms. Jeanne DeFazio for her kind help.

感谢Jeanne DeFazio女士的热心帮助。

Silly, Silly Mouse
Jamie Book 2

杰米传奇 (第二卷)

Silly, Silly Mouse Jamie Book 2

CONTENTS

1. How Many weBPets Does Jamie Get? 4
2. Can Jamie Tell Left From Right? 28
3. Can A Genius Play the Piano without Practicing? 48
4. The Most Prayerful Mouse in the World? 66
5. Little Mice Amy and Drew 84
6. Are All the Fish in the Lake Frozen? 102
7. Can Jamie Fix Everything with Duct Tape? 118
8. Does the Tooth Fairy Exist? 134
9. Can Jamie Sky-Dive without a Parachute? 150
10. Can Jamie Walk in the Fire? 168

杰米传奇（第二卷）

目 录

1. 杰米拥有多少个网络宠物？ 5
2. 杰米能分清左右吗？ 29
3. 天才钢琴家不需要练琴吗？ 49
4. 世界上最爱祷告的老鼠？ 67
5. 小老鼠艾米Amy和德烈Drew 85
6. 湖里的鱼被冻住了吗？ 103
7. 杰米能用胶带修好一切吗？ 119
8. 牙仙存在吗？ 135
9. 杰米不需要降落伞就能空降吗？ 151
10. 杰米能在火里行走吗？ 169

1. HOW MANY WEBPETS DOES JAMIE GET?

"I am the smartest mouse in the world," said the little white mouse Jamie at a toy store. "I want to own all 1,500 weBPets. The more, the better. I will become the biggest fan on the weBPets website."

"Jamie, that giant fan looks way bigger than you," said the little gray mouse Andrew as he pointed to a big paper fan hanging on the wall.

"I'm not talking about a paper fan," said Jamie. "I mean the biggest hobbyist."

1. 杰米拥有多少个网络宠物？

"我是世界上最聪明的老鼠。"小白鼠杰米在玩具店里说,"我希望拥有所有 1,500 个网络宠物(weBPets),越多越好。我会成为网络宠物网站上的最大的 fan。"

"杰米,那把大扇子 fan 比你大多了,"小灰鼠安德烈说,他指着挂在墙上的一把大纸扇。

"I see," said Andrew. "Why do you want to have so many weBPets? I think one is good enough for me."

"You are such an old-fashioned mouse! " said Jamie while he hugged 12 weBPets. "weBPets are the most popular stuffed animals. There are 1,500 different types of them. For example,

there are 200 different kinds of dogs among them. Everyone in my Sunday school class owns one. Each animal has a code for you to register on the website. You can take care of them online like taking care of real pets."

Jamie and Andrew went home from the toy store with 13 new weBPets.

"我说的不是纸扇子,"杰米说,"我的意思是最大的爱好者。"

"哦,我明白了,"安德烈说,"你为什么想得到那么多网络宠物呢?我想,对我来说一个就足够了。"

"你真是个思想老旧的老鼠啊!"杰米说,一面用胳膊拥抱了12个网络宠物。"网络宠物是现在最流行的毛绒动物玩具。共有1500种不同的动物玩具。比如说其中有200种不同的小狗。我主日学班上每个孩子都有一个。每个动物有一个代码,你可以在网站上注册。你可以在网上象照顾真的宠物一样照顾他们。"

杰米和安德烈买了13个网络宠物,从玩具店回家。

"我会在我的房间里吃晚餐,"杰米说着。他一手抓了块比萨饼,另一手提着玩具袋。"我今晚感谢上帝赐给我12个网络宠物和这块比萨饼。阿们!"

"I am going to eat my dinner in my room," said Jamie while he grabbed a slice of pizza with one hand and held the toy bag in the other hand. "I thank God for giving me these 12 weBPets and one slice of pizza tonight. Amen."

Jamie ran upstairs to his room and left the rest of the family at the dining table.

"What is Jamie doing?" asked Jamie's owner Jack. "He isn't eating dinner with us. This has never happened before."

"I think he is taking care of his 12 new pets," said Andrew.

"12 new pets?" asked Jack. "Which pets has he got? I think two mice are enough for our family."

"He bought an elephant, tiger, lion, penguin, monkey, panda, and a giraffe," said Andrew. "He also got a zebra, crocodile, cat, horse, and dog, but I only bought a whale."

"You mean toy pets," said Jack. "I don't think Jamie wants to keep a cat or a crocodile in his room. I don't think a real elephant or giraffe would fit in his room anyways."

"Yes, they are stuffed animals," Andrew said, and took his weBPet whale out of his pocket. "However, you take care of them on the weBPets website. You can feed them, play with them, buy new clothes for them, and take baths for them.

杰米跑上楼，进了他的房间，把其余的家人留在餐桌旁。

"杰米在做什么呀？"杰米的主人男孩捷克问道，"他没有跟我们一起吃晚餐。这从来没有发生过。"

"我想他正在照顾他的 12 个新宠物，"安德烈说。

"12 个新宠物？"捷克说，"他得到了哪些新宠物呢？我觉得我们家有两只宠物老鼠就足够了。"

"他买了大象，老虎，狮子，企鹅，猴子，熊猫，长颈鹿，"安德烈说，"他还得到了斑马，鳄鱼，猫，马，狗。但我只买了一条鲸。"

"你的意思是玩具宠物，"捷克说，"我不认为杰米想要在他的房间里养一只猫或者一条鳄鱼。我也不认为一只真正的大象或长颈鹿能塞进他的房间。"

"是啊！它们是毛绒玩具，"安德烈从兜里拿出他的网络宠物鲸，"不过，你必须在网络

Jamie told me if you missed one meal for them, they would die."

"Really?" said Jack. "Let's see what will happen with Jamie."

Eight days later, the family talked about Jamie at the dining table again.

"Jamie has behaved oddly since he got his weBPets," said Jack. "He hasn't eaten dinner with us for eight days. He took my computer and I cannot do my homework."

"He also took my computer," said Jack's sister, Sally.

"An online toy store sent me a bill of $24,000!" yelled Dr. Charlie while he opened an envelope. "That's more expensive than my car. We need to investigate this."

"I think that Jamie has probably spent the money on his toys," said Andrew. "I found ten big boxes in our backyard. The labels on the boxes showed the name of the online toy store. By the way, my computer is also missing. I can only use Jack's smart phone to play with my weBPet whale on line ."

"I couldn't find my smart phone anywhere the whole week," said Mother Anna.

"Jack and Andrew, could you go ask Jamie about what he did?" asked Dr. Charlie.

宠物网站上照顾它们。你必须喂它们食物，和它们一起玩、为它们买新衣服、并为它们洗澡。杰米告诉我，如果你少喂它们一顿饭，它们就可能会死。"

"真的吗？"捷克说，"让我们看看杰米会怎么样。"

八天以后，全家人在餐桌上再次谈到杰米。

"杰米自从买了网络宠物以后，表现古怪，"捷克说，"他整整一周都没有和我们一起吃晚餐。他拿走了我的电脑。我都没法做作业。"

"他也拿走了我的电脑，"捷克的姐姐莎莉说。

"一个网上玩具店寄给我 24,000 美元的账单！"爸爸博士查理打开一个信封的时候突然大喊，"这比我的车还贵。我们要调查这件事。"

"我想杰米大概把钱花在网络宠物上了，"安德烈说，"我在后院发现了 10 个大箱子。箱

Silly, Silly Mouse Jamie Book 2

Jack and Andrew went upstairs and knocked at Jamie's door.

They heard Jamie say, "Come in!"

As soon as Jack opened the door, many stuffed animals tumbled into the hallway. Before Jack could say anything, Andrew was already buried under the pile of stuffed animals.

子的标签上有网上玩具店的名称。顺便说一下，我的电脑也不翼而飞。我只能用捷克的智能手机来上网跟我的宠物鲸玩。"

"我一个星期都找不到我的智能手机，"妈妈安娜说。

"捷克和安德烈，你们能去问问杰米做了什么吗？"查理博士问道。

捷克和安德烈上楼去敲杰米的门。

他们听到杰米说："进来吧！"

捷克一打开门，许多毛绒动物玩具就掉到走廊上。捷克还没来得及说话，安德烈已经被埋在一堆玩具下面。

"安德烈，你在哪里？"捷克喊着。

"我在这里，"安德烈喊着说，他爬出玩具堆，头上还有两只玩具猫。

捷克向安德烈伸手。安德烈沿着捷克的手臂爬到他的肩膀上。

捷克和安德烈往杰米的房间里观看。房间看上去像装满毛绒动物的游泳池，堆了有两英

"Andrew, where are you?" shouted Jack.

"I'm here," called Andrew as he climbed out the toys with two stuffed animal cats on his head.

Jack reached out his hand to Andrew. And the mouse ran along Jack's arm onto his shoulder.

Jack and Andrew looked inside Jamie's room. The room looked like a swimming pool full of stuffed animals piled two feet high. There were weBPets on Jamie's bed, desk, dresser, bookshelf, and some even hung on the lights.

"Wow," exclaimed Andrew. "Am I dreaming that I am inside weBPet Land?"

"I think Jamie ordered the weBPets from the online toy store," said Jack. "This can explain the big boxes in our backyard and the huge bill."

They spotted Jamie sitting on his chair by his desk. Then each of Jamie's hands was typing on the keyboards of two laptop computers on his desk. His feet were typing on two other computers on the floor. His tail was typing on the keyboard of a smart phone. There were piles of dirty dishes on his desk.

"Look, our computers and phones are here," said Andrew.

"Jamie, what are you doing?" asked Jack.

"I'm working hard to feed my weBPets," replied Jamie without turning his head. "I only have

尺厚。杰米的床、书桌、柜子、书架上都是网络宠物，甚至在灯上还挂了几个。

"哇，"安德烈惊呼，"我是在做梦进了网络宠物乐园吗？"

"我想杰米从网上玩具店订购了网络宠物，"捷克说，"这就可以解释后院的大箱子和巨额账单了。"

他们看到杰米坐在书桌边的椅子上。杰米的手在桌子上的两台笔记本电脑键盘上打字。他的脚在地板上的两台电脑的键盘上。他的尾巴在按智能手机的键盘。书桌上有成堆的脏盘子。

"你看，我们的电脑和手机都在这里，"安德烈说。

"杰米，你在做什么呀？"捷克问道。

"我在辛苦地喂我的网络宠物，"杰米头也不转地回答他们，"我只有一分钟时间来喂一个网络宠物，所以我不得不每天工作 24 小时。这样我就能每天喂一次我的 1500 个网络宠物中的 1440 个。"

one minute to feed one weBPet, so I have to work 24 hours a day. Then I will be able to feed 1,440 out of 1500 weBPets each day."

"I play with my whale weBPet 5 minutes a day," said Andrew. "My whale not only eats, but also takes a bath and plays with me. He is healthy and happy."

"Jamie, how about the rest of your 60 weBPets?" asked Jack.

"They may starve," said Jamie. "They have to sleep 24 hours a day."

"Poor weBPets," Andrew said as he shook his head. "Your weBPets must be hungry and sad."

Jack slowly found his way through the toys to Jamie's desk with Andrew on his shoulder.

"Jamie, look at the status of your weBPets," said Jack while he pointed to the computer screen. "You have 1,500 weBPets, and you are ranked number one among the weBPets fans. However, 60 of your weBPets never ate anything. 720 weBPets never took a bath, and the other 720 never played games with you. Your weBPets are hungry, dirty, and sad. You are not taking good care of them at all."

A message suddenly appeared on the screen. "Game over! You have played more than 183 hours on this website. Your account has expired,

"我每天跟我的鲸玩 5 分钟，"安德烈说，"我的鲸，不但吃得饱，洗了澡，还和我玩。他又健康又快乐。"

"杰米，剩下的 60 个网络宠物怎么办呢？"捷克问道。

"他们也许会饿死，"杰米说，"他们只能每天 24 小时睡觉。"

"可怜的网络宠物，"安德烈说着，抹着眼泪，"你的网络宠物一定又饥饿又悲哀。"

捷克费力地走过玩具，向杰米的书桌走去。安德烈在他的肩膀上。

"杰米，看看你网络宠物的状态，"捷克说着，一面指着电脑屏幕，"你一共有 1500 个网络宠物。你在网络宠物网站上的爱好者里排名第一。然而，你的 60 个网络宠物从来没有吃任何食物。720 网络宠物从来没有洗过澡，剩下 720 从来没有和你玩过。你的网络宠物又饥饿，又肮脏，又悲哀。你根本没有好好照顾他们。"

and you have lost all of your weBPets. You have been kicked out of the weBPets community."

"Oh no!" cried Jamie as he banged his fists on the keyboards angrily. "My 1,500 weBPets! I was the biggest fan in the weBPets community, but now I have zero weBPets."

"Why did that happen?" asked Jack.

"A person should only play on this website for half an hour each day," said Andrew. "Then that person can play for one year. But Jamie has used all his hours during the past 8 days."

"I want to buy another 1,500 weBPets," said Jamie as he cried. "I am going to the online toy store now."

"Stop!" cried Jack. "Jamie, you have already wasted $24,000 dollars. Look at what you've been doing for the past 8 days. You've been addicted to the game all day. There are big boxes in our yard. You have taken other peoples' computers and smart phones. This is too crazy! We can't let you do this anymore."

"I'll wash dishes and clean up our house to pay back the money," said Jamie. "I am bankrupted."

"Jamie, if you earn one dollar each day for doing chores," said Andrew as he pressed the buttons on a calculator, "you will have to do that for the next 66 years."

杰米传奇（第二卷）

突然，一条信息出现在屏幕上："游戏结束。您在本网站已经玩了超过 183 小时。您的帐户已过期。您已经失去了所有网络宠物。您已被踢出网络宠物社区。"

"哦，不！"杰米哭着，疯狂地用拳头打键盘，"我的 1500 个网络宠物呀！我是网络宠物社区最大的爱好者，但我现在只有 0 个网络宠物啦！"

"为什么会发生这样的事呢？"捷克问道。

"一个人每天只能上这个网站半小时，"安德烈说，"这样就可以玩一年。但杰米在过去 8 天里已经把所有的时间都用完了。"

"我想另外再买 1500 个网络宠物，"杰米一面说一面哭，"我现在要去网上玩具店。"

"停下来！"捷克喊着说，"杰米，你已经浪费了 24,000 美元。看看你在过去的 8 天里都做了什么。你整天整夜沉迷于游戏。在我们的后院里有很多大箱子。你拿走了别人的电脑

"I'll also mow the lawn every week," said Jamie, "so I can pay back 5 dollars each week."

"Then it will take only 39 years," said Andrew, "Even if you mow the lawn on snowy days."

"What should I do now?" asked Jamie. "I am so disappointed in myself."

"Jamie, don't be worried," said Dr. Charlie at Jamie's door, "I have an idea. I'm going to a fund-raising auction party for wild animal protection tonight. I think your full collection of weBPets might sell well."

"Yes!" Jamie said excitedly. "I am the smartest mouse in the world. Some of my weBPets have become rare. My weBPets may be the only full collection in the world. We might make a fortune out of them. Dr. Charlie, you can take them! I love the wild animals."

Jack, Andrew and Jamie cleaned up the stuffed animals in Jamie's room, put them into ten plastic bags, and carried them to Dr. Charlie's car.

Late at night, Dr. Charlie came home.

"Daddy, did you sell all the weBPets?" asked Jack.

"Yes!" said Dr. Charlie excitedly as he waved a check in his hand, "A gentleman paid $120,000 for our toys. So we got our money back and I donated the earnings to a wild animal foundation."

和智能手机。这太疯狂啦！我们不能让你再这样做了。"

"我会洗碗和打扫房子来还钱，"杰米说，"我现在负债累累了。"

"杰米，你做家务能每天得到一美元，"安德烈一面说一面按着计算器，"你将不得不做66年的家务。"

"我也会每周修剪草坪，"杰米说，"这样我每个星期可以还5美元。"

"这将减少到39年，"安德烈说，"即使下雪天你也修剪草坪的话。"

"现在我应该怎么做呢？"杰米说，"我对自己太失望啦！"

"杰米，不要担心，"查理博士在杰米的房门口说，"我想出了一个主意。我今晚要去参加为保护野生动物筹款的拍卖会。我想你的网络宠物完整收藏有可能卖个好价钱。"

"对！"杰米很兴奋，"我是世界上最聪明的老鼠。我的一些网络宠物已成为珍稀藏品。我的网络宠物毛绒动物可能是世界上唯一的完

"You see," said Jamie, "my weBPets are helping the real animals."

"Dr. Charlie, why do I still see the big bags in your car?" asked Andrew.

"Later, that gentleman decided that he didn't want the stuffed animals," said Dr. Charlie, "so he gave them back to me."

"Wow!" said Jamie happily, "My weBPets are back!"

"We can donate them to the kids in need," said Dr. Charlie. "Tomorrow, we are going to give away mittens and scarves in the city."

整收藏。我们可以靠卖它们来发财。查理博士,把它们都拿去吧!我爱野生动物。"

捷克、安德烈和杰米清理了杰米的房间里的毛绒动物,放到 10 个塑料袋里,并扛到查理博士的汽车里。

深夜,查理博士回到家。

"爸爸,你卖掉网络宠物了吗?"捷克问道。

"是的!"查理博士激动地说,一面挥舞着一张支票,"有位绅士为我们的玩具支付了 12 万美元。因此,我们的钱回来了。我把赚的部分捐给了野生动物基金会。"

"你看,"杰米说,"我的网络宠物能帮助真正的动物。"

"查理博士,为什么我看到那些大袋子还在你的车里呢?"安德烈问道。

"后来,那位绅士不想要毛绒玩具,"查理博士说,"所以他把它们还给了我。"

"哇!"杰米说,"我的网络宠物回来啦!"

"I love this idea!" said Jack.

"I can also give away my whale weBPet," said Andrew.

"That's not a bad idea," said Jamie.

The next day, the family went to a park in the city to give mittens and scarves to the people in need. Jamie and Andrew were in charge of giving the weBPets to the kids.

"What a beautiful weBPet lion!" said a boy happily as he got a weBPet from Jamie. "Thank you, little mouse."

"You're welcome," said Jamie, smiling. "Take good care of your toy."

"I love this weBPet panda," said a little girl as Jamie gave her a toy. "It looks so cute. You are a great hero, little mouse!"

"Thank you," said Jamie. "Enjoy your stuffed animal."

After the activity, Andrew said, "we gave away 1501 weBPets to 1501 kids!"

"I have never felt so happy in my life!" said Jamie. "My greed for toys never made me feel satisfied. I never knew that I could make 1501 kids smile."

"我们明天可以把它们捐赠给有需要的儿童,"查理博士说,"明天我们要去市中心发放手套和围巾。"

"我喜欢这个主意!"捷克说。

"我也可以捐赠我的网络宠物鲸,"安德烈说。

"这个主意还不错。"杰米说。

第二天,全家人在市中心的公园分发手套和围巾给有需要的人。杰米和安德烈负责分发网络宠物给小孩子们。

"这个网络宠物狮子真好看,"一个男孩说,他从安德烈手里接过一个网络宠物,"谢谢你,小老鼠。"

"不客气,"安德烈说,"好好照顾你的玩具哦。"

"我喜欢这个网络宠物大熊猫,"一个小女孩说着,杰米给了她一个玩具,"它看起来很可爱。你是一个大英雄,小老鼠。"

"谢谢你,"杰米说,"好好玩你的毛绒动物。"

Discussion Questions and Activities:

1. Why did Jamie want to be the biggest fan of the weBPets?
2. What odd behaviors has the family observed about Jamie when he was playing on the weBPets website?
3. How did Jamie get his 1500 weBPets?
4. Did Jamie take care of his weBPets well?
5. How did Dr. Charlie solve the money problem?
6. How did the weBPets make the kids smile?
7. Memorize Proverbs 28:25, "A greedy man stirs up strife, but the one who trusts in the Lord will be enriched."

杰米传奇（第二卷）

活动结束后，安德烈说，"我们赠送了 1501 个网络宠物给 1501 个小孩子。"

"我从来没有感到那么高兴过，"杰米说，"我对玩具的贪心从来没有使我感到过满足。我从来不知道我能使 1501 个小孩子微笑。"

讨论问题和活动：

1. 为什么杰米要做网络宠物最大的爱好者？
2. 全家人发现杰米有哪些怪异的行为？
3. 杰米是如何得到他的1500个网络宠物的？
4. 杰米好好照顾他的网络宠物了吗？
5. 查理博士是如何解决债务问题的？
6. 网络宠物怎样使小孩子们微笑？
7. 请背诵经文《箴言》28:25 "心中贪婪的，挑起争端。倚靠耶和华的，必得丰裕。"

2. CAN JAMIE TELL LEFT FROM RIGHT?

"There were more than 120,000 people in Nineveh who could not tell their right hand from their left hand," said the little gray mouse Andrew. "That is a big number, ten times of the population in our town."

"Those people are really silly!" said the little white mouse Jamie, holding out his palms. "They can't even tell left from right. It's so easy."

One Friday night, Dr. Charlie, Mother Anna, Sally, Jack, Jamie, and Andrew were studying the Bible. They were studying Chapter 4 of the book

2. 杰米能分清左右吗？

"在尼尼微有超过 12 万人分不清他们的左右手,"小灰鼠安德烈说,"这是一个很大的数字,有我们镇上人口的十倍呀!"

"那些人是太傻了!"小白鼠杰米伸出他的双手,"他们连左右手都分不清楚。这多简单啊!"

一个星期五晚上,爸爸查理博士,妈妈安娜,姐姐莎莉,弟弟捷克,小白鼠杰米和小灰

of Jonah, about how God loves people who can not tell apart their left and right hands. Jamie laughed about those people.

"Those people are babies," said Jack.

"I even know several adults who cannot tell their left hand from right hand," said Sally.

"Really?" asked Jamie.

"Once I taught a visiting professor to drive a car," said Dr. Charlie. "Whenever I told him to turn left, he always turned right."

"That's funny," said Andrew.

"I even know an eighty-year old grandma who mixed up her left and right hands," said Mother Anna. "If we have wrong concepts about our faith from the beginning, it would be difficult to correct them all our lives."

"I am the smartest mouse in the world," said Jamie. "I will never make a misnake about such a simple concept."

"Misnake? Ha ha!" Andrew laughed. "Jamie, it is 'mistake', not 'misnake'. You made a mistake when you first learned the word 'mistake'."

"When you miss a snake," said Jamie, "you make a misnake. What's wrong with that?"

"Okay, kids," said Mother Anna, "it's time to go to sleep. Don't forget : all of you have to get up early to go to the amusement park tomorrow morning."

鼠安德烈一起在家里学圣经。他们读到约拿书第 4 章关于上帝爱惜分不清左右手的人。杰米嘲笑了这些人。

"这些人是婴儿。"捷克说。

"我还认识几个分不清左右手的成年人呢。"莎莉说。

"真的吗?"杰米问道。

"有一次,我教一位来访问的化学教授开车,"查理博士说,"每当我告诉他向左转,他总是向右转。"

"太可笑啦!"安德烈说。

"我甚至认识一位八十岁的老奶奶,她的左手和右手搞混了。"安娜说,"如果我们对信仰一开头就有错误观念,将来就会很难纠正。"

"我是世界上最聪明的老鼠,"杰米说,"我绝不会对这样一个简单的概念犯误错。"

"误错?哈哈!"安德烈大笑,"杰米,这是'错误',而不是'误错'。当你第一次学这个词'错误'的时候,你就犯了一个错误。"

The next morning, Sally, Jack, Jamie and Andrew went to the amusement park.

At the park, they had a mini car race. The path was complicated, and the racers had to figure out the correct path. Jamie drove with Jack as a team. Andrew drove with Sally as the other team. They put on their helmets, jumped into the cars with open tops, and put their seatbelts on. Sally and Jack guided them by reading the maps.

Jamie said, "I am the best mouse racer in the world. We will surely beat them."

The race began. Jamie stepped on the gas pedal and his car rushed out.

"Bye-bye!" Jamie waved his hand to Andrew. Andrew's car was soon far behind.

Soon, Jamie and Jack's car arrived at the first intersection.

Jack looked at the map and said, "The Rainforest is on the right. So we should turn right here."

Jamie nodded and said, "No problem. I will turn right." However, he turned the car left.

Jack shouted, "What are you doing, Jamie? I told you to turn right, but you turned left!"

Jamie argued, "Look! I turned right. Is there anything wrong?"

Jack said, "You turned left!"

"当你无错的时候，"杰米说，"你就会犯一个误错。这有什么错？"

"好啦，孩子们，"母亲安娜说，"该睡觉啦。别忘了你们明天还要早起去游乐园。"

第二天早晨，莎莉、捷克、杰米和安德烈去了游乐园。

在公园里，他们先去参加赛车。路径很复杂，车手要找出正确的道路。杰米和捷克是一个团队，杰米开车。安德烈和莎莉是另一队。他们戴上头盔，跳上敞篷车，系好安全带。莎莉和捷克担任向导，看地图。

杰米说，"我是世界上最优秀的老鼠赛车手。我们一定能打败他们。"

比赛开始，杰米一踩油门，车就冲了出去。

"再见！"杰米向安德烈挥手。安德烈的车被远远抛在后面。

不久，杰米和捷克的车到达第一个岔路口。

Jamie waved his left hand and said, "What are you talking about? I turned to the right hand direction."

Jack's eyes widened and he said, "Now I understand! You mixed up your left and right hands from whenever your learned this concept."

Jamie looked at his left hand and said, "Really? Is this my left hand? Oops, I've made this misnake for all my life! We have to drive back!"

Just before Jamie finished his words, the car rushed into the Rainforest. Rain started pouring into the car and drenched the car. Jamie and Jack were soaked as if they just went swimming.

Jamie tried to turn around, but the car was stuck in mud. Jamie and Jack climbed out of the car to push it out of the mud.

Suddenly a monkey jumped down from a tree.

"What? A monkey?" Jamie said, his eyes widening, "What is he going to do?"

The monkey said in a robotic voice, "I am here to help you to push the car."

"Oh! The monkey is a robot," said Jamie, smiling.

Together they pushed the car out of the mud. After thanking the monkey, Jamie and Jack drove back to the first intersection.

Andrew and Sally's car was still behind.

捷克看着地图说,"向左转会到热带雨林。所以,我们应该在这里右转。"

杰米点点头,说:"没问题。我会在这里右转。"然而,他立即把车左转。

捷克大喊,"杰米,你在做什么呀?我告诉你右转,但是你却左转!"

杰米说,"瞧!我向右转了呀。有什么不对吗?"

捷克说:"你向左转了呀!"

杰米挥着他的左手说:"你说什么呀?我转向了右手的方向呀!"

捷克的眼睛睁得老大,"现在我明白了,当你第一次学左右手这个概念的时候,你就把左右手弄反了。"

杰米看着自己的左手,说:"真的吗?这是我的左手?糟糕,我原来一直犯了这个误错。我们得开回去!"

杰米话还没说完,车子就冲进了热带雨林。雨水进了车,车里很快就灌满了水。杰米

Jamie clapped his hands, saying, "We are totally going to win!"

Jamie went to the right way. Soon, they reached the second intersection.

Jack looked at the map and told Jamie, "Bear Mountain is on the left. We should turn left here."

Jamie said, "Okay!" and immediately turned to the right hand direction.

Jack yelled, "Jamie, you made the same MISNAKE again!"

Jamie waved his right hand and said, "No, this is the left hand direction."

Jack shook his head and said, "That is your right hand."

和捷克全身都湿了,好像是掉进了一个游泳池。

杰米试图倒车,但车陷在泥里。杰米和捷克从车里爬出来推车。

突然,一只猴子从树上跳了下来。

"什么?一只猴子?"杰米很惊讶,"他要干什么呀?"

猴子用机器人的声音说:"我来帮助你们推车。"这个猴子原来是一个机器人。他们一起把车推出来。谢过猴子后,杰米和捷克开车返回到第一个十字路口。

安德烈和莎莉的汽车仍然在他们身后。

杰米拍拍手,说:"我们一定会赢得这场比赛!"

这个时候,他们转向正确的方向。不久,他们到达第二个十字路口。

捷克看着地图对杰米说:"熊山在右手方向。我们要在这里左转。"

杰米说:"好!"立刻把车向右转。

"Really?" Jamie said, his eyes widening. "Oops. It is really difficult to correct this habit in a short period of time."

They quickly arrived at Bear Mountain. A tall black bear ran close to the car. Jamie was scared and drove his car around. The bear chased them and his paw almost reached Jamie's helmet. Finally, the bear took hold of the rear bumper of

the car. The car could not move even when Jamie stepped hard on the gas pedal. Suddenly the bear's eye flashed, and a photo came out of a slot on his chest.

The bear said in a robotic voice, "Welcome to Bear Mountain."

捷克喊道:"杰米,你又犯了同样的'误错'!"

杰米挥右手,说:"没错啊,这是左手方向啊。"

捷克摇着头,说:"那是你的右手。"

"真的吗?"杰米的眼睛睁得老大,"糟糕。短时间内真是很难纠正这种习惯。"

他们很快到达熊山。一个高大的黑熊跑到汽车边。杰米吓得开着车乱转。熊追赶他们,熊的爪子几乎够着杰米的头盔。最后,熊抓住汽车的后保险杠。尽管杰米使劲踩油门,车子还是动弹不得。突然熊的眼睛闪光,一张照片从他胸口上的槽里弹出来。

熊用机器人的声音说:"欢迎来到熊山。"

"熊竟然是一个机器人摄影师,"杰米说,"他把我吓坏了。这下我总算松了一口气。"

"照片看起来很可笑,"捷克看着照片说,"我们大张着嘴,看起来被吓坏了。"

他们开车回到第二个十字路口。

"The bear is a robotic photographer," said Jamie. "He scared me. Now I feel relieved."

"The photo looks funny," said Jack as he looked at the photo. "We look really scared- look, our mouths are open and our eyes are wide."

They drove back to the second intersection.

"Look, Andrew and Sally's car is still behind us," said Jamie as he drove to the correct direction.

Quite soon, Jamie and Jack's car reached the third intersection.

Jack told Jamie, "We should turn to the right hand direction here. There is a waterslide and a Crocodile Pond on the left hand direction."

"Okay!" Jamie replied. "I won't make the same misnake this time." So he turned to the right hand direction.

Jack yelled, "This is the wrong direction!"

Jamie waved his right hand and said, "What's the problem? You told me to turn to the right hand direction, and I did it. Look at my palm. I secretly wrote the letter R on my right hand. I will never make the same misnake again."

Jack cried, "Sorry. I told you the opposite direction on purpose. I was worried that you might make the mistake again."

While they were talking, their car fell down the waterslide.

"看哪,安德烈和莎莉的车还在后面,"杰米说着,向正确的方向行驶。

不久,杰米和捷克的汽车达到第三个路口。

捷克告诉杰米说:"我们应该向右转。左手方向有滑水道和鳄鱼池。"

"好的!"杰米回答说:"这次我不会再犯误错了。"于是,他把车转向右手方向。

捷克喊道:"这是错误的方向!"

杰米挥着右手说:"有什么问题?你告诉我向右转,我照着做了。你看我的掌心。我偷偷地在我右手心里写上了'右'字。我再也不会犯同样的误错了。"

捷克哭了,"对不起。我故意告诉你相反的方向,因为我很担心你可能会再次犯同样的错误。"

他们正说着话,汽车就冲下了滑水道。

杰米和捷克尖叫着,仅仅抓住扶手。车滑下滑水道的速度非常快,左右摆动。杰米和捷

Jamie and Jack screamed and held the car tightly. The car slid down the slide very fast, swinging left and right. Jamie and Jack shook left and right, up and down. They closed their eyes.

Finally, the car splashed into a pond.

"The pond isn't deep," said Jack. Jamie and Jack's heads were out of the water, although the car was underwater.

"We are still okay, let me drive the car out of the pond," said Jamie while he stepped on the gas pedal.

He looked around and observed a crocodile, with a big mouth and shiny teeth, was swimming towards the back of the car.

Jamie yelled, "Help! A crocodile is coming!" He stepped hard on the gas pedal. The car moved forward, but the crocodile kept chasing them. Soon the crocodile bit the rear bumper of the car.

Jamie asked Jack, "What should we do now?"

The crocodile spoke with a robotic voice, "I am here to help you out of the pond."

"The crocodile is also a robot," said Jack.

The crocodile pushed the car out of the pond. Jamie and Jack thanked the crocodile and drove towards the finish line.

克也左右、上下地摇动。他们尖叫着,闭上了眼睛。

最后,车冲进了一个池塘。池塘不深。杰米和捷克的头伸在水外面,汽车在水里。

"我们还行,让我把车开到池塘外。"杰米一面说一面踩油门。

他环顾四周,发现一只大鳄鱼,张着大嘴,牙齿闪亮,向车后游过来。

杰米大叫:"救命啊!鳄鱼来了!"他使劲踩油门。车向前移动。但鳄鱼还在追着他

When they arrived at the finish line, they found that Sally and Andrew had already won the race.

Jamie cried, "We could have won the game if I were able to tell left from right."

Jack said, "Jamie, take it easy! The game is for fun, not for winning. You have corrected your confusion about left and right today. Now you will know it all your life and never make this misnake again."

"Yes!" said Jamie. "Mistake. M-I-S-T-A-K-E."

们。不久，鳄鱼咬住车的后保险杠。杰米问："现在我们怎么办？"

鳄鱼用机器人的声音："我来帮助你们开出池塘。"原来是个机器鳄鱼。

鳄鱼把车推出池塘。杰米和捷克感谢了鳄鱼，驱车朝着终点线开。

当他们到达终点线时，他们发现莎莉和安德烈已经赢得了比赛。

杰米哭了："如果我能分清左右手，我们就可以赢得比赛了。"

捷克说："杰米，别太在意！赛车是个快乐的游戏，不是为了输赢。今天你纠正了左右的概念，你就会一辈子都不再犯这个'误错'了。"

"是啊！"杰米说，"错误。错-误-。"

Discussion Questions and Activities:

1. Find the Bible verse Jonah 4:11. Who are the people who cannot tell their left hand from their right hand?
2. Can you tell left from right?
3. Do you know anyone who mixes up their left and right hands?
4. Why did Jamie turn to the wrong direction at the first intersection?
5. Why did Jamie turn to the wrong direction at the second intersection?
6. Why did Jamie turn to the wrong direction at the third intersection? Whose fault is it this time?
7. Is it important for Jamie to win the race? If you fail in a chess game or a swimming contest, what should your attitude be?
8. What's the message of this story?
9. Memorize Hebrews 5:13-14, "For everyone who lives on milk is unskilled in the word of righteousness, since he is a child. But solid food is for the mature, for those who have their powers of discernment trained by constant practice to distinguish good from evil."

杰米传奇（第二卷）

讨论问题和活动：

1. 请阅读《圣经》约拿书，第四章讲的"分不清左右手的人"指的是什么人？
2. 你能分清左右手吗？
3. 你认识混淆了左右手的人吗？
4. 为什么杰米在第一个十字路口转错了方向？
5. 为什么杰米在第二个十字路口转错了方向？
6. 为什么杰米在第三个十字路口转错了方向？这次是谁的错？
7. 杰米赢得比赛很重要吗？如果你在一个国际象棋比赛或游泳比赛失败了，你的态度应该怎样？
8. 这个故事的中心思想是什么？
9. 请背诵经文《希伯来书》5:13-14，"凡只能吃奶的，都不熟练仁义的道理。因为他是婴孩。惟独长大成人的，才能吃干粮。他们的心窍，习练得通达，就能分辨好歹了。"

3. CAN A GENIUS PLAY THE PIANO WITHOUT PRACTICING?

"I hate playing the piano," complained the little white mouse Jamie while he was chewing bubble gum and juggling 3 balls. "Which is the most boring activity in the world! It's a job for a robot. I am the smartest mouse in the world. I don't want to do this silly practicing."

"Jamie, if you want to play beautiful music," said Jack, "you have to practice thousands of times. There is no other way, even for a genius."

"I enjoy playing the piano," said the little gray mouse Andrew. "I don't think pianists behave

3. 天才钢琴家不需要练琴吗？

"我讨厌弹钢琴，"小白鼠杰米抱怨道，他一面嚼着泡泡糖，一面扔着三个杂耍球，"那是世界上最无聊的事情！那是机器人干的工作。我是世界上最聪明的老鼠。我不想做这种愚蠢的练习。"

"杰米，如果你想演奏优美的音乐，"捷克说，"你就得练习上千次。即使是一个天才，也没有别的办法。"

like robots. They are great musicians, and I admire them a lot."

Every time when Jack asked Jamie to play the piano, they always had the same fight. However, Andrew practiced for two hours a day, and he could play very long and difficult pieces. Jamie only practiced five minutes a day. So he could only play simple songs like *Mary Had a Little Lamb* with one hand.

"The talent show in our school will take place in one month," said Jack. "Both of you can play the piano. Sally will play the violin and I will play the guitar. You'd better practice hard. Jamie, put down your juggling balls and go to play the piano now."

Jamie spit his gum into the trash can. He kept juggling while whistling *Mary Had a Little Lamb* and walked back to his room.

"Jamie might be a genius," said Andrew. "However, he is just too lazy."

"I'm really worried about his performance in the talent show," Jack sighed as he shook his head.

One minute later, the music *Joshua Fought the Battle of Jericho* came out of Jamie's room.

"This sounds really great!" Jack said with a smile.

"我喜欢弹钢琴,"安德烈说,"我不认为钢琴家表现得像机器人。他们是伟大的音乐家,我很佩服他们。"

每次当捷克让杰米弹钢琴的时候,就会有这样的争斗。与此相反,安德烈每天练琴两个小时。他可以弹很长很难的作品。然而,杰米每天只练习五分钟。他只会用一只手弹简单的音乐,像"玛丽有只小羊"。

"我们学校的才艺表演将在一个月后举行,"捷克说。"你们两个都要弹钢琴。莎莉会拉小提琴,我会弹吉他。你们最好现在开始苦练。杰米,放下你的杂耍球,现在去弹钢琴。"

杰米把口香糖吐到垃圾桶里。他一面扔杂耍球,一面吹着口哨"玛丽有只小羊",走回自己的房间。

"杰米可能是一个天才,"安德烈说,"他只是太懒啦。"

"我真的很担心他的才艺表演,"捷克摇了摇头,叹了口气。

"He is a genius! I always know that, because I am his best friend," said Andrew.

The music kept coming out of Jamie's room.

After a while, Andrew looked at the clock, and said, "He played for half an hour."

"Amazing! Jamie never played the piano for

such a long time," said Jack. "He seems serious now."

"I know he can do it," said Andrew.

Jamie came out of his room, still whistling and juggling. However, he was whistling *Joshua Fought the Battle of Jericho* this time.

"You did a great job, Jamie!" Jack said and gave Jamie a piece of chocolate. Jamie didn't stop jug-

一分钟以后,"约书亚打耶利哥之战"的音乐从杰米的房间里传出。

"这听起来确实不错啊!"捷克面带微笑地说。

"他是个天才!我一直知道这件事,因为我是他最好的朋友。"安德烈说。

音乐从杰米的房间里传出来。

一段时间后,安德烈看了看时钟说,"他弹了半小时。"

"真是不可思议啊。杰米从来没有弹过这么长的时间的钢琴。"捷克说,"看起来这一次他终于严肃对待了。"

"我知道他能做得很好。"安德烈说。

杰米走出了他的房间,仍然吹着口哨和扔着杂耍球。然而,这次他吹的是"约书亚打耶利哥之战"。

"你干得非常出色,杰米!"捷克说着,给了杰米一块巧克力。杰米没有停止扔杂耍球,却把嘴伸到捷克的手里吃了巧克力。

gling the balls, but reached Jack's hand with his mouth.

"Jamie, we are proud of you!" said Andrew. "You will surely give a great show!"

Chewing the chocolate, Jamie went back to his room without saying anything, still juggling the balls.

The same music came out of Jamie's room for another hour.

Jack and Andrew were very happy with Jamie's progress.

Every day, Jack and Andrew heard music coming out of Jamie's room for two hours. Sally, Jack, and Andrew were also practicing hard in their own rooms.

The night before the talent show, Andrew secretly told Jack, "Jack, I found that Jamie is really a genius. This afternoon, I saw Jamie coming out of his room juggling balls, but the piano in his room was still playing. I think he must have some magic power."

"Really?" said Jack. "That's hard to believe! Let's have a rehearsal tonight."

That night, Sally, Jack, Andrew and Jamie had a rehearsal.

First, Sally played the violin music *Who Built the Ark?* Everybody applauded.

"杰米,我们为你感到骄傲!"安德烈说,"你的演出一定会很成功!"

杰米嚼着巧克力,回去他的房间,什么都没有说,还是扔着杂耍球。

同样的音乐从杰米房间又传出一个小时。

捷克和安德烈对杰米的进步感到非常高兴。

每天,捷克和安德烈听到音乐从杰米的房间传出两个小时。莎莉、捷克和安德烈也在自己的房间里苦练音乐。

才艺表演前一天晚上,安德烈偷偷告诉捷克,"捷克,我发现杰米真是一个天才啊。今天下午,我发现杰米走出他的房间扔着杂耍球,但是他房间里的钢琴还在弹。我想他一定有某种神奇的能力。"

"真的吗?"捷克说,"真让人难以置信!我们今晚预演一下。"

那天晚上,莎莉、捷克、安德烈和杰米预演了节目。

Next, Jack also played *Who Built the Ark*, except with the guitar. Although he played very well, everyone said, "It would be boring to hear the same music twice in one talent show." Jack was very upset.

After that, Andrew played the piano. Surprisingly, Andrew also played *Who Built the Ark?*. Everybody was very disappointed.

"We will look very silly to play the same song three times," said Sally. "People can easily tell we didn't communicate with one another at all."

"Although everyone of us have worked very hard for a whole month," said Andrew, "without proper communication, all of our efforts are wasted."

"We will look really bad before the whole school," Jamie said. "Every student will make jokes on us, singing 'Who built the ark? Dr. Charlie's family! Dr. Charlie's family!'"

"Jamie, we are counting on you," Jack said, and patted Jamie on his shoulder.

Jamie started to play the piano. The audience heard *Joshua Fought the Battle of Jericho*. It sounded fabulous. They applauded.

"Jamie, you are our life-saver," said Jack.

"Thank you! Thank you!" Jamie stood up from the piano bench and bowed to the audience like a great pianist.

首先，莎莉演奏小提琴乐曲"谁建了方舟？"大家都鼓掌。

其次，捷克演奏吉他，还是"谁建了方舟？"。尽管他弹得非常好，大家说，"在一个才艺表演中两次听到同样的音乐会让人觉得很枯燥。"捷克很是懊恼。

第三，安德烈弹钢琴。令人惊讶的是，安德烈弹的还是同样的音乐。每个人都非常失望。

"我们三次演奏同样的音乐，看起来真的很傻，"莎莉说，"人们可以很容易看出我们没有彼此沟通。"

"虽然我们每个人都非常努力地练习了整整一个月，"安德烈说，"由于没有适当的沟通，我们的所有努力都白费了。"

"我们会在全校面前显得非常糟糕。"杰米说，"每一个学生都会笑话我们，唱'谁造了方舟呀？查理博士的家庭！博士查理的家庭！'"

One weird thing happened. They heard the music playing once again while Jamie was not sitting in front of the piano.

"You see, I said Jamie has some magic power," said Andrew.

One little black box slipped out of the top pocket on Jamie's shirt. The audience found the music came from the box. Jack picked up the box and found it is a digital voice recorder.

"Jamie, you cheated on us for a month!" said Jack. "You were just playing music from the voice recorder. You never practiced at all."

"We are a total failure," Sally cried. "The talent show will take place tomorrow. What should we do now?"

"Jamie, I thought you were a genius with some magic power," Andrew also cried. "How can you cheat on us? We are your family."

"It is my fault to have cheated everyone," Jamie said, bursting into tears. "But I really hate practicing the piano."

"We suck!" said Jack. "Three of us practiced the same song, while the other one did not practice at all."

"We are a family," said Sally. "Instead of blaming each another, we should take responsibility together. When Noah's family built the ark, they loved one another and worked together. If they

"杰米，我们这次就指望你啦。"捷克说，拍拍杰米的肩膀。

杰米开始弹钢琴。听众们听到音乐"约书亚打耶利哥之战"。这音乐听起来很美妙。观众们鼓起掌来。

"杰米，你真是救了我们的命。"捷克说。

"谢谢！谢谢！"杰米从钢琴凳边站起来，像一个伟大的钢琴家一样向听众鞠躬。

一件奇怪的事情发生了。尽管杰米不是坐在钢琴前，听众们却听到同样的音乐再次响起。

"看，我说过杰米有神奇的力量。"安德烈说。

一个黑色小盒子从杰米的衬衫口袋滑落在地。观众发现音乐是从小盒子里传出来的。捷克拿起盒子，发现它是一个数码录音机。

"杰米，你欺骗了我们一个月！"捷克说，"原来你是从录音机里播放音乐。你根本没有练琴。"

could not work together, they would never build the ark. Don't be worried! I have a great idea!"

"What a great idea! Let's do it now!" Everybody applauded after hearing Sally's idea.

The next night, at the school talent show, when it is time for Sally to perform, people were amazed to see that Sally, Jack, Jamie and Andrew went onto the stage together.

Sally was playing the violin, Jack was playing the guitar, and Andrew was playing the piano. How about Jamie? He juggled 3 balls on the stage. They performed as a band.

The announcer said, "Next is Sally, Jack, Jamie and Andrew. They will present *Who Built the Ark?*

The music came up, and Jamie sang, "Who built the ark? Noah, Noah," while juggling 3 balls.

"我们完全失败了。"莎莉泪流满面,"明天就是才艺表演。我们现在怎么办呢?"

"杰米,我以为你是一个有神奇能力的天才,"安德烈也哭了,"你怎么能骗我们呢?我们是你的家人呀。"

"欺骗大家是我的错,"杰米眼泪流了出来,"但我真的很讨厌练钢琴。"

"太糟糕啦!"捷克说,"我们三个人练了同样的乐曲,而另外一个根本就没有练。"

"我们是一家人,"莎莉说,"与其互相指责,不如我们来共同承担责任。你知道,当诺亚的家庭建方舟的时候,他们彼此相爱共同努力。如果他们不同心,他们永远建不成方舟。不要担心!我有一个好主意!"

"真是个好主意!我们现在就开始做吧!"听到莎莉的想法后,大家都鼓掌。

第二天晚上,在学校的才艺表演会上,当轮到莎莉表演的时候,人们惊奇地看到,莎莉,捷克,杰米和安德烈一起上了舞台。

He even did a cartwheel on the stage while singing.

All the audience applauded and shouted "Great music! Great singing! We love it! Now we know who built the ark."

Note: The song '*Who built the ark*' was composed by Jeff Reeves.

杰米传奇（第二卷）

莎莉演奏小提琴，捷克演奏吉他，安德烈弹钢琴。杰米呢？他在舞台上玩三个杂耍球。他们作为一个乐队来演出。

播音员说："下一个节目是莎莉、捷克、杰米和安德烈。他们要表演'谁建了方舟？'"

音乐响起来，杰米唱道："谁建了方舟呀？诺亚，诺亚。"他同时在玩杂耍球。他甚至边唱边在舞台上做侧身翻。

所有的观众鼓掌高呼："美妙的音乐！唱得太好啦！我们太喜欢啦！现在我们知道是谁建了方舟啦！"

注：歌曲"谁建了方舟"是由 Jeff Reeves 所作。

Discussion Questions and Activities:

1. Why didn't Jamie like playing the piano?
2. Did Andrew like playing the piano?
3. Did Jamie really practice hard?
4. How did Jamie cheat and why?
5. Did the four friends communicate well for the show? How did they finally give the show?
6. What talent did Jamie show on the stage?
7. Learn to sing the song *Who Built the Ark?*
8. What would you do when your parents ask you to practice playing the music instruments?
9. Memorize Proverbs 26:16, "The sluggard is wiser in his own eyes than seven men who can answer sensibly."
10. Memorize 1 John 4:12, "No one has ever seen God; if we love one another, God abides in us and his love is perfected in us."

杰米传奇（第二卷）

讨论问题和活动：

1. 为什么杰米不喜欢弹钢琴？
2. 安德烈喜欢弹钢琴吗？
3. 杰米真的辛苦练琴了吗？
4. 杰米怎样欺骗大家的，他为什么这样做？
5. 这四个朋友在才艺表演前有很好沟通吗？他们最终是如何表演的？
6. 杰米在舞台上展现了什么样的才能？
7. 学唱歌曲"谁建了方舟？"
8. 当你的父母要求你练习演奏乐器时，你会怎样做？
9. 请背诵经文《箴言》26:16 "懒惰人看自己，比七个善于应对的人更有智慧。"
10. 请背诵经文《约翰一书》4:12："从来没有人见过神。我们若彼此相爱，神就住在我们里面，爱他的心在我们里面得以完全了。"

4. THE MOST PRAYERFUL MOUSE IN THE WORLD?

"Now I lay me down to sleep. I pray to Lord, my soul to keep. The angel mice watch me through the night. I happily wake in the morning light. Amen," prayed the little white mouse Jamie.

The little gray mouse Andrew started laughing. "Ha! Jamie, you made a mistake!"

"Jamie, we asked you to say our grace," said Jack. "We're not going to sleep at our dining table."

4. 世界上最爱祷告的老鼠?

"现在我躺下睡觉。请求上帝保守我的灵魂。天使小鼠整夜看顾我,直到我在晨光中醒来。阿们!"小白鼠杰米在祷告。

"哈哈!杰米,你祷告错了!"小灰鼠安德烈说。

"杰米,我们让你做谢饭祷告。"捷克说。"我们不打算在餐桌边睡觉。"

Silly, Silly Mouse Jamie Book 2

This happened one night before dinner. It was Jamie's turn to pray for the whole family, but he made a mistake by saying a bedtime prayer.

"Sorry! Sorry, everyone!" said Jamie, "Let me pray again. It is my habit to give that bedtime prayer every night."

"Dear Lord," prayed Jamie, "Thank You for giv-

ing us food. Please bless Dr. Charlie, Mother Anna, Sally, Jack, Andrew and myself. In Jesus' name we pray, Amen."

杰米传奇（第二卷）

这件事发生在晚餐桌边。轮到杰米做谢饭祷告，但他却错误地做了睡前祷告。

"抱歉，抱歉，对不起大家！"杰米说，"让我再祷告一次。我每天晚上做睡前祷告。这是我的习惯。"

"亲爱的主，"杰米祈祷，"感谢您给我们食物。求你保守查理博士、安娜、莎莉、捷克、安德烈和我自己。我们奉耶稣的名字祷名，阿们。"

"杰米，谢谢你的祈祷！"查理博士和妈妈安娜说。杰米已经开始吃饭。

"杰米，你的祷告太烦人了！"安德烈抱怨说，"每次当你做谢饭祷告，你说的都是同样的话。"

"安德烈，我是世界上最爱祷告的老鼠，"杰米说。"上帝喜欢听我从心底发出的祷告。"

"杰米，你只会做这两个祷告，"安德烈说，"我甚至可以把每个字都背出来。你在过去的两年里每天祷告完全一样。我想上帝也可

"Jamie, thank you for your prayer!" said Dr. Charlie and Mother Anna while Jamie started eating.

"Jamie, your prayer is too boring!" said Andrew. "Every time when you give our grace, you say exactly the same prayer."

"Andrew, I am the most prayerful mouse in the world," said Jamie. "God loves listening to my prayers which come from the bottom of my heart."

"Jamie, you only pray these two prayers," said Andrew. "I can even memorize every word of them. You have prayed exactly the same every day for the past two years. I think God might also feel bored about your prayers. No mouse wants to receive exactly the same phone call from another mouse every day."

"Jamie, it is okay!" said Anna. "Take it easy. We love you."

"We love you, Jamie!" said Dr. Charlie and Sally.

"Jamie and Andrew," said Jack, "finish your dinner first. Then let's study the Bible to learn how to pray."

After dinner, Jack led the Bible study with Andrew and Jamie.

"We are going to study the Lord's Prayer today!" said Jack.

能对你的祷告都烦了。没有一只老鼠想每天收到从另一只老鼠来的完全相同的电话。"

"杰米,没关系!"安娜说,"别太在意!我们都爱你。"

"我们都爱你,杰米!"查理博士和莎莉说。

"安德烈和杰米,"捷克说,"先把饭吃完,然后我们可以一起学圣经。"

晚饭后,捷克带领安德烈和杰米一起学圣经。

"我们今天来学习主祷文!"捷克说。

"我会背诵!"杰米说。

"我也会!"安德烈说。

"我们在天上的父,愿人都尊你的名为圣。愿你的国降临。愿你的旨意行在地上,如同行在天上。我们日用的饮食,今日赐给我们。免我们的债,如同我们免了人的债。不叫我们遇见试探,救我们脱离凶恶。因为国度、权柄、荣耀,全是你的,直到永远,阿们。"杰米和安德烈一起背诵道。

"I can recite it!" said Jamie.

"Me, too!" said Andrew.

"Our Father in heaven, hallowed be your name. Your kingdom come, your will be done, on earth as it is in heaven. Give us today our daily bread, and forgive us our debts, as we also have forgiven our debtors. And lead us not into temptation, but deliver us from the evil one. For yours is the kingdom, and the power, and the glory forever. Amen," Jamie and Andrew recited together.

"Great job!" said Jack. "Today, we are going to learn how to pray a balanced prayer, which is called an A-C-T-S prayer."

Jack held up his left hand.

"Adoration," Jack said, and pointed to his pointer finger.

"Confession," Jack said, and pointed to his middle finger.

"Thanksgiving," Jack said, and pointed to his ring finger.

"Supplication," Jack said, and pointed to his pinky. "So, A, C, T, S. Do you remember that there is a book in the Bible called *Acts*?"

"That is a nice way to memorize this!" Andrew said excitedly.

"Easy!" said Jamie. "Adoration, Confession, Thanksgiving, and Supplication. That is ACTS."

"背得太好啦！"捷克说。"今天，我们要学习祷告。一个平衡的祷告是所谓 ACTS 祷告。"

捷克伸出他张开的手。

"敬拜。"捷克指着他的左手食指。

"认罪。"捷克指着他的左手中指。

"感恩。"捷克指着他的左手无名指。

"祈求。"捷克指着他的左手小指。"因此，A，C，T，S。你还记得有《圣经》里有一卷书叫 Acts《使徒行传》？"

"这是一个帮助记忆的好办法！"安德烈很兴奋。

"这太容易啦！"杰米说，"敬拜，认罪，感恩和祈求。这是 ACTS。"

杰米给捷克和安德烈看他的左手，他已经把这四个字母写在四个手指上。

"这是一个提醒自己的好办法。"捷克说："杰米，你可以做个包含这四个方面的祷告吗？"

Jamie also showed Jack and Andrew his left hand. Jamie already wrote the four words on his four fingers.

"That is an excellent way to remind yourself," said Jack. "Jamie, could you give a prayer with these four points?"

"Okay!" said Jamie. "Dear Lord, thank You for giving us food."

"Ha!" Andrew laughed. "You made the same mistake again."

"Sorry!" said Jamie. "Let me try again. Dear Lord, we praise you for your glory and your love. We thank you for creating us. Thank you for giving us eternal life. I confess that I did not pray too often. I pray your kingdom come. Bless my best friends Jack and Andrew. In Jesus' name, Amen."

"What a great prayer!" said Jack. "Your prayer contains all the four ACTS."

Jamie really liked praying. He prayed many times a day, counting the letters written on his fingers.

One day, Jamie and Andrew were playing around the swimming pool in the backyard of their house.

Suddenly, Jamie fell into the swimming pool.

"好的！"杰米说，"亲爱的主，感谢您赐给我们食物。"

"哈哈！"安德烈说，"你再次犯了同样的错误。"

"抱歉！"杰米说，"让我再做一遍。亲爱的主，我们赞美您的荣耀和你的爱。我们感谢您创造了我们。感谢您赐给我们永恒的生命。我承认，我没有做太多的祈祷。我祈祷您的国降临。求您保守我最好的朋友捷克和安德烈。奉耶稣的名祷告，阿们。"

"真是一个伟大的祷告！"捷克说。"你的祷告包含了这四个要点 ACTS。"

杰米真的很喜欢祈祷。他每天祈祷很多次，数着写在他的手指上的字母。

有一天，杰米和安德烈在他们房子后面的游泳池边玩耍。

突然，杰米掉到游泳池里。

"亲爱的上帝，您能派一位天使来救我吗？"杰米一面在水中挣扎，一面祈祷。

"Dear God, could you please send an angel to rescue me?" prayed Jamie, while struggling in the water.

"Jamie, don't worry," said Andrew. "Let me get Jack to rescue you."

"You don't have to! I am waiting for an angel to rescue me," said Jamie. "God loves listening to my prayers."

Andrew ran to look for Jack.

Ten seconds later, Andrew came back with Jack. Jack tried to reach Jamie with a long stick.

"Jamie, hold on to the stick," said Jack. "You will be rescued."

"杰米，不用担心，"安德烈说，"我去叫捷克来救你。"

"不需要！"杰米说，"我要等天使来救我。上帝喜欢听我的祷告。"

安德烈跑去寻找捷克。

10秒后，安德烈和捷克一起回来。捷克拿了根棍子伸向杰米。

"杰米，抓住棍子，"捷克说，"你就能被救出来啦。"

"我不需要它。"杰米一面说一面拍打着水，"我在等待天使来拯救我。现在，我要做ACTS祷告。"

杰米看着写在他的手指上的四个字母，开始祷告，"亲爱的主，我赞美你的爱和你的荣耀。我承认我今天在游泳池边走不太小心。我感谢你让我浑身都湿了，这样我就可以节省一些淋浴水。您能送一位天使来救我的命吗？"

他继续拍打着水。

安德烈把一艘遥控船放到游泳池里。他按了遥控器上的按钮。船向杰米行驶。

"I don't need it," said Jamie while striking the water. "I am waiting for an angel to rescue me. I will do the ACTS prayer now."

Jamie looked at the four letters on his fingers, and started to pray, "Dear Lord, I praise your love and your glory. I confess that I did not walk carefully by the pool today. I thank you for making me wet, so I can save some shower water. Could you please send an angel to save my life?"

He kept kicking the water.

Andrew pushed a remote control ship into the pool. He pressed the buttons on the remote control. The ship cruised towards Jamie.

"Jamie, I am sending a ship to rescue you!" said Andrew.

"I do not need it," said Jamie. "I believe God will send an angel…"

Jamie sank underwater before he finished his words.

Jack dived into the swimming pool. He searched underwater and found Jamie. Jack grabbed Jamie's arm and came out of the water. Jack swam to dry land and put Jamie onto the ground.

Jamie was unconscious.

Jack pressed Jamie's chest and blew air into Jamie's mouth.

Jamie spit out water and opened his eyes.

"杰米，我送了一只船来救你！"安德烈说。

"我不需要它，"杰米说，"我相信上帝会派天使…"

杰米话还没说完就沉下了水。

捷克跳到游泳池里。他在水下搜索，发现了杰米。他抓住杰米的胳膊，浮出水面。捷克游回来，把杰米放在地上。

杰米晕倒了。

捷克按压杰米的胸部，对杰米的口里吹气。

杰米吐出水，睁开眼睛。

"我在天堂里吗？"杰米问。

"傻老鼠！"安德烈说，"你差点没命了。"

"我很高兴你醒过来了，"捷克说，"你仍然在我们的家，还没有上天堂。"

"我以为天使会来救我，"杰米说，"我拼命祷告。为什么天使没来救我？"

"Am I in heaven now?" asked Jamie.

"Silly mouse!" said Andrew. "You almost lost your life."

"I am so happy you woke up," said Jack. "You are still at our home, not in heaven yet. We cannot lose you."

"I thought an angel would have come to rescue me," said Jamie. "I prayed hard. Why didn't the angel come?"

"I want to jump back to the pool, so I can see an angel from God saving my life," Jamie said. He stood up, about to jump back into the pool.

"Stop! Don't jump!" Jack and Andrew said while running over to pull Jamie's arms.

"Jamie," said Jack, "when we pray to God, God will do what people cannot do. We can save you, so God sent us to save your life."

"But it is different from what I prayed," Jamie cried.

"Yes!" said Jack. "It's different from what you thought, but that's God's way."

"Probably God didn't hear my prayer," said Jamie.

"God surely did!" said Jack. "That's why you are saved! Your prayer has been answered."

"Praise the Lord!" Jamie said, stopped struggling and smiled.

"我想跳回到游泳池里，"杰米站了起来，走到池边，想跳回池里，"这样我就可以看到上帝派来的天使来救我啦。"

"停下来！不要跳！"捷克和安德烈跑过来拉着杰米的胳膊。

"杰米，"捷克说，"当我们向上帝祈祷，上帝能做我们不能做的事。我们可以救你，上帝就派我们来救你。"

"但这和我祷告的不一样啊，"杰米哭了。

"是啊！"捷克说，"这和你想的不一样，但这是上帝的方式。"

"可能是上帝没有听到我的祷告。"杰米说。

"上帝肯定听到了！"捷克说，"这就是为什么你得救了！你的祷告已经得到上帝的垂听。"

"赞美主！"杰米停止了挣扎，笑了起来。

Discussion Questions and Activities:

1. How many prayers does Jamie have?
2. Can you recite the Lord's Prayer (Matthew 6:13-19)?
3. What are the parts of the ACTS prayer?
4. Why didn't Jamie want to be saved by Jack and Andrew when he fell into the swimming pool?
5. Why did Jamie want to jump back into the pool?
6. Does God always answer our prayer exactly as we prayed?

杰米传奇（第二卷）

讨论问题和活动：

1. 杰米有多少个祷告词？
2. 你能背诵主祷文（马太福音6:13-19）吗？
3. 什么是ACTS的祷告？
4. 杰米掉到游泳池里，为什么他不希望捷克和安德烈来救他？
5. 为什么杰米想跳回池中？
6. 我们祈祷的时候，上帝总是垂听我们的祈祷吗？

5. THE LITTLE MICE AMY AND DREW

"Jamie, where is the letter 'J' on your sweater?" the little gray mouse Andrew shouted to the little white mouse Jamie.

"The letter 'J'? It is still on my chest," said Jamie as he pointed to his chest and looked down.

"Oops!" Jamie cried as he ran to a mirror. "It disappeared."

This happened one morning at breakfast. Andrew found that the letter 'J' on Jamie's sweater was missing. All of Jamie's sweaters have a big

5. 小老鼠艾米AMY和德烈DREW

"杰米，你毛衣上的字母'J'到哪里去了？"小灰鼠安德烈对小白鼠杰米大喊。

"字母'J'？它还在我胸前啊！"杰米一面说一面指着自己胸前，低头往下看。

"哎呀！"杰米大叫，跑到镜子前，"它消失了。"

这件事发生在一天早晨，吃早饭时，安德烈发现，杰米毛衣上的字母"J"不见了。杰

letter 'J' on the chest. Of course, all of Andrew's sweaters have a big letter 'A'.

"Somebody stole the letter 'J' from my sweater," Jamie shouted.

"You're not Jamie anymore. You're Amy now," said Andrew.

"You're not Andrew anymore. You're Drew now," said Jamie.

"What?" Andrew looked down at his own chest and shouted, "The letter 'A' on my sweater is also missing!" Andrew also ran to the mirror.

"What on earth has happened here?" asked Andrew.

米所有的毛衣胸前都有一个大大的字母"J"。当然，安德烈的所有毛衣上都有大大的字母"A"。

"有人偷走了我毛衣上的字母'J'。"杰米喊道。

"你现在不是'杰米'(Jamie) 了。你现在是艾米(Amy)，"安德烈说。

"你现在不是'安德烈'(Andrew) 了。你现在是德烈(Drew)。"杰米说。

"什么？"安德烈向下看自己的胸口，他惊奇地发现在他毛衣上的字母"A"也不翼而飞。安德烈也跑到镜子前。

"到底发生了什么事？"安德烈说。

"这是我经历过的最惊人的事情，"杰米说。"也许，一个小偷半夜进入了我们的卧室，偷走了我们的的字母？"

"艾米，这不可能，"安德烈说。"为什么一个小偷想偷我们毛衣上的字母呢？他能拿去卖钱吗？"

"This is the most surprising thing that has ever happened in my life," said Jamie. "Maybe a thief sneaked into our bedrooms at midnight and stole our letters?"

"Amy, that's impossible," said Andrew. "Why would a thief want to steal the letters on our sweaters? Can he sell them to make money?"

"Drew, don't call me Amy," said Jamie. "That's a girl's name. If the letters were not stolen by a thief, could they be stolen by an alien?"

"Sorry, I will just call you Jamie," said Andrew. "But I don't think aliens even exist. Even if aliens exist, can they use the superpower inside our letters to drive their flying saucer?"

"If the letters were not stolen by a thief or an alien, the letters might be somewhere in our house," said Jamie. "Let's look for them all over the house."

"Not a bad idea," said Andrew.

The two little mice started looking for the letters everywhere inside the house.

They checked the laundry baskets, but didn't find any clues. They checked the closets in their bedrooms and threw out all of their clothes, but the letters on those clothes did not disappear.

Their bedrooms were messy with clothes everywhere on the floor.

"Where could our letters be?" asked Andrew.

"德烈，不要叫我艾米，"杰米说，"这是一个女孩的名字。如果字母不是被一个小偷偷走了，难道是被外星人偷走的吗？"

"对不起，我还是叫你杰米吧！"安德烈说，"我不相信外星人存在。即使外星人存在，他们能用我们字母中的超级能量来驱动他们的飞碟吗？"

"如果字母没有被小偷或者外星人偷走，字母可能会在我们家里的某个地方，"杰米说，"让我们满屋子找找。"

"这主意不坏，"安德烈说。

两个小老鼠开始在家里到处寻找字母。

他们检查了洗衣篮，但没有发现任何线索。他们在自己卧室检查壁橱，把所有衣服都抛出来，也没有找到任何线索。

他们把卧室弄得乱七八糟，地板上到处是衣服。

"到底字母在哪里呢？"安德烈说。

"捷克告诉过我们，"杰米说，"我们应该向上帝祷告寻求帮助。"

"Jack once told us that we should pray to the Lord for help," said Jamie.

Jamie and Andrew knelt down in the hallway to pray. "Dear Lord," they said, "could you please tell us what happened to our letters and how to get them back?"

"What are you two doing here?" asked Jack when he saw the two mice kneeling in the hallway.

"We are praying," said Jamie. "The letters on our sweaters are missing. Do you know who took them?"

"Nope," said Jack. "But Sally might know. Let's go to ask Sally."

Jack knocked at Sally's door.

"What's going on here?" Sally asked as she opened her door.

"Jamie and Andrew cannot find the letters on their sweaters," said Jack.

"You may ask Mommy," said Sally. "She washed their sweaters."

Jack and two mice went to the kitchen to ask Mother Anna.

"Poor little mice!" said Anna. "Be patient and think. I believe you will find them. You can also ask your daddy."

Dr. Charlie just came in.

"亲爱的主，"安德烈和杰米在走廊里跪下来祈祷。"您能否告诉我们字母发生了什么事，如何让他们回来？"

"你们两个在这里做什么呢？"捷克问，当他看到两只老鼠跪在走廊上。

"我们在祷告，"杰米说，"我们的毛衣上的字母不见了。你知道是谁把他们拿走了吗？"

"不是我，"捷克说。"莎莉可能知道。我们一起去问问莎莉吧！"

捷克敲了莎莉房间的门。

"这是怎么回事？"莎莉打开门问道。

"杰米和安德烈找不到自己毛衣上的字母，"捷克说。

"你去问妈妈吧！"莎莉说，"她洗过他们的毛衣。"

捷克和两只小老鼠去厨房问妈妈安娜。

"可怜的小老鼠！"安娜说。"要有耐心，好好想一想。我相信你们会找到它们的。你们也可以去问爸爸。"

"Daddy, Daddy!" said Jack. "Jamie and Andrew cannot find the letters on their sweaters. Could you help them?"

"Really?" said Dr. Charlie. "Let me think."

Dr. Charlie looked at Jamie and Andrew's sweaters carefully.

"I've figured it out!" said Dr. Charlie with a smile. "But I won't tell you. It's like a riddle. I want you to figure it out by yourself."

Dr. Charlie left them while smiling.

"That is very weird," said Jack. "How come Daddy can figure it out just by looking at you two?"

"We don't know," said Jamie and Andrew.

"Let me also look at both of you carefully," Jack said and looked at the two mice up and down.

The two mice looked confused.

"Turn around," Jack said.

The two mice turned around.

"I have also figured it out," said Jack as he laughed.

"Jack, tell us! Please!" said Jamie. "Don't play the riddle with us anymore. We are upset enough."

"Just go to the mirror and turn around," said Jack. "Observe carefully."

查理博士正好走了进来。

"爸爸,爸爸!"捷克说,"杰米和安德烈找不到自己毛衣上的字母。你能帮助他们吗?"

"真的吗?"查理博士说,"让我想想。"

查理博士仔细观察杰米和安德烈身上的毛衣。

"我明白了!"查理博士面带微笑地说,"但我不会告诉你们。这就好像是一个谜语。我想要你们自己来解开这个谜。"

查理博士微笑着离开他们走了。

"这太奇怪了,"捷克说,"为什么爸爸看看你们两个就明白了呢?"

"我们不知道呀,"杰米和安德烈说。

"让我也仔细看看你们两个。"捷克说着,上下看着两只小老鼠。

两只老鼠被搞糊涂了。

"转身,"捷克说。

两只小老鼠转身。

"我也明白啦。"捷克说着大笑起来。

Jamie and Andrew went to look into the mirror and turned around. They observed carefully.

"I know what has happened!" Jamie said and jumped up and down.

"Tell me! Tell me!" said Andrew.

"Look carefully!" said Jamie. "Especially look at the stitches on your sweater."

Andrew looked into the mirror carefully.

"It's so weird," said Andrew. "How come the stitches are outside of my sweater? They should be inside."

"Now you figure it out!" said Jamie.

"We are wearing our sweaters INSIDE OUT!" shouted Andrew as he laughed. "That is really silly!"

Jamie and Andrew took off their sweaters and ran to Jack.

"Jack! Jack!" said Jamie and Andrew. "We've figured out what happened!"

They turned their sweaters inside out and put them back on.

"It was very silly for us to look for the letters all around," said Jamie. "We thought it was something difficult."

"We should look into our mirror more often," said Andrew.

"Jamie!" Jack said to Andrew.

"I'm not Jamie," said Andrew.

"捷克,告诉我们吧!"杰米说,"不要让我们再猜谜语啦。我们已经够心烦的了。"

"去镜子面前转身,"捷克说,"仔细观察。"

杰米和安德烈去镜子面前转身,仔细地观察。

"我知道发生什么事啦!"杰米说着上蹦下跳。

"告诉我,告诉我!"安德烈说。

"仔细看!"杰米说,"特别是毛衣上的缝线。"

安德烈仔细照镜子。

"太奇怪啦!"安德烈说,"为什么我的毛衣缝线会在外面?它们应该在里面。"

"现在你明白了吧!"杰米说。

"我们把毛衣内外穿翻了!"安德烈说。"这真的太傻啦!"

杰米和安德烈脱下自己的毛衣,向捷克跑去。

"Andrew!" Jack said to Jamie.

"I'm not Andrew," said Jamie.

"Go to look into the mirror again," said Jack.

Jamie and Andrew ran back to the mirror. They looked into the mirror and laughed.

"It is silly of you to wear my sweater," Jamie told Andrew.

"You are even sillier," said Andrew. "You're wearing my sweater."

"It is easy to talk about looking into the mirror," said Jack. "But we really need to keep the Biblical words in our heart and examine our mind and behavior all the time."

Jamie and Andrew took off the sweaters and swapped.

"We have been busy for the whole morning but didn't do anything," said Jamie. "We should've been more patient and more careful."

"What a lesson we've learned!" exclaimed Andrew.

The next morning, the whole family was eating breakfast.

Jamie and Andrew stared at Dr. Charlie's sweater.

They suddenly shouted, "Dr. Charlie, you're wearing your sweater inside out!"

Everybody looked at Dr. Charlie.

"Really?" Dr. Charlie said, looking awkward.

"捷克！捷克！"杰米和安德烈说。"我们明白了！"

他们把自己的毛衣翻过来，再穿上。

"我们到处去找字母实在是太傻啦！"杰米说。"我们还以为是件很困难的事呢。"

"我们应该更经常照镜子，"安德烈说。

"杰米！"捷克对安德烈说。

"我不是杰米。"安德烈说。

"安德烈！"捷克对杰米说。

"我不是安德烈。"杰米说。

"再去照照镜子。"捷克说。

杰米和安德烈跑回镜子面前。他们照着镜子，笑了起来。

"你穿着我的毛衣，太傻啦，"杰米对安德烈说。

"你更傻，"安德烈说，"你穿着我的毛衣。"

"照镜子说着容易，"捷克说，"我们确实需要把圣经的话语藏在心里。经常检查我们自己的思想和行为。"

He ran to the mirror. His face turned red as he said, "Really!"

He took off his sweater, turned it inside out and put it back on, and said, "Everybody can make this simple mistake. I didn't look into the mirror this morning."

"Yes!" said Jamie and Andrew. "Everybody makes mistakes. However, if we look into our mirror more often, we can always make corrections."

杰米和安德烈脱掉了毛衣,交换回来。

"我们整个上午都在无事忙,"杰米说。"我们本来应该更有耐心,更仔细。"

"我们真是学到了一个教训啊。"安德烈说。

第二天早晨,全家人都在吃早餐。

杰米和安德烈瞪着查理博士的毛衣。他们突然喊道:"查理博士,您把毛衣内外穿翻了!"每个人都看着查理博士。

"真的吗?"查理博士看起来很尴尬。他跑到镜子面前。他红着脸说:"真的!"

他脱下毛衣,翻过来穿上,说:"每个人都会犯这个简单的错误。我今早没有照镜子。"

"是的!"杰米和安德烈说:"每个人都会犯错误。可是,我们如果经常照镜子,总是可以纠正错误。"

Discussion Questions and Activities:

1. Why did Andrew laugh at Jamie in the morning?
2. Were the letters on the sweaters stolen by a thief or an alien?
3. Did Jack, Sally, or Anna know where the letters were?
4. How did Dr. Charlie figure out the problem?
5. Did Jamie and Andrew finally figure out the problem?
6. Why did Jack Andrew "Jamie"?
7. Memorize Proverbs 25:2, "It is the glory of God to conceal things, but the glory of kings is to search things out."

杰米传奇（第二卷）

讨论问题和活动：

1. 为什么早上安德烈笑话杰米？
2. 毛衣上的字母是被小偷或着外星人偷走了吗？
3. 捷克、莎莉和妈妈安娜知道字母在哪里吗？
4. 查理博士是如何找出问题？
5. 杰米和安德烈最终解决问题了吗？
6. 为什么捷克把安德烈称为杰米？
7. 请背诵经文《箴言》25:2 "将事隐秘，乃神的荣耀。将事察清，乃君王的荣耀。"

6. ARE ALL THE FISH IN THE LAKE FROZEN?

"Let's go ice fishing!" said Jack.

"What a great idea!" said the little gray mouse Andrew.

"I love fishing," said the little white mouse Jamie. "I'm the best fisher-mouse in the world."

One cold winter day, Jack, Jamie, and Andrew decided to go ice fishing on the lake. They put on their winter coats.

Jack grabbed two fishing poles and asked Jamie, "Jamie, could you get the hammer and chisel?"

6. 湖里的鱼被冻住了吗？

"我们去冰钓吧！"捷克说。

"好主意！"小灰鼠安德烈说。

"我喜欢钓鱼，"小白鼠杰米说，"我是世界上最优秀的老鼠渔夫。"

在冬季寒冷的一天，捷克、杰米和安德烈要去湖上冰钓。他们穿上冬装。

捷克拿了两根钓鱼竿。他告诉杰米拿上锤子和凿子。

"Why do we need them?" Jamie asked.

"We need to break the ice," said Jack.

"The lake is frozen," said Jamie excitedly. "So all the fish in the lake must be frozen into this gigantic piece of ice. We only need to cut the ice to get the frozen fish inside."

"You will see," Jack laughed.

When they arrived at the lake, they found the whole lake was covered with ice.

They carefully walked to the center of the lake.

"Let's dig here," said Jack.

"Okay!" said Jamie.

Jamie knelt down to cut the ice with his hammer and chisel. He cut a circular piece of ice, picked it up and looked at it through the sun light.

"I am so disappointed," said Jamie. "There is no frozen fish in the ice!"

"Look!" said Jack as he pointed to the hole on the ice. "There is water in the hole. Fish can swim under the ice."

"I believe I will be able to find frozen fish in the ice if I work hard enough," said Jamie. "I just haven't found the right location."

"Fish don't get frozen inside the ice," said Jack as he cast his fishing rod into the hole.

"为什么我们需要这些工具？"杰米问。

"我们需要打破坚冰，"捷克说。

杰米兴奋地说："湖被冻住了。湖里所有的鱼就会被冻在这块巨大的冰块里。我们只需要打破冰，就能得到里面的冻鱼啦。"

"你会明白的，"捷克笑着说。

当他们到达湖边的时候，他们发现湖面被冰覆盖。

他们小心翼翼地走到湖中心。

"我们在这里挖吧！"捷克说。

"好的！"杰米说。

杰米跪在冰面上，用锤子和凿子开始破冰。他切开一个圆形冰块，拿起冰块对着阳光看。

"真让人失望！冰里面没有冻鱼呀！"杰米说。

"瞧，"捷克指着冰面上的洞说，"冰下面有水。鱼可以在冰下游泳啊。"

"I want to try again," said Jamie. "You two can fish here. I will try to cut the ice in other places."

So Jamie went to another location on the ice and cut another circle in the ice. He picked up the ice block and looked into it.

"What a big disappointment," Jamie said to himself. "There is no frozen fish inside. If I try harder, I will be able to find fish."

He worked hard and dug many holes in the ice, but never found any fish in the ice.

Finally, he picked up one piece of ice and saw a frozen fish inside.

"Jack! Jack!" Jamie shouted from far away. "I found a fish inside the ice!"

"我相信只要我足够努力，我一定能在冰里找到冻鱼，"杰米说，"我只是还没有找到正确的位置。"

"鱼不会被冻在冰里的。"捷克一面说一面把鱼线和鱼钩放到洞里。

"我想试试。"杰米说，"你们两个可以在这里钓鱼。我去别的地方破冰看看。"

杰米去到另一个位置的冰上，开始在冰切割一个圆圈。他拿起冰块来看。

"太让人失望啦！"杰米说，"里面没有冻鱼。如果我加倍努力，我一定能够找到鱼。"

他努力地在冰面上挖了许多洞，却没有发现任何鱼。

最后，他拿起一块冰，看到冰里有一条冻鱼。

"捷克！杰克！"杰米远远喊着，"我在冰里发现了一条鱼。"

"那肯定是在冰形成以前就死了的鱼。"捷克一面大声回喊，一面拿着他的钓竿。

"That must be a fish that died before the ice formed," Jack shouted back while holding his fishing pole.

"Let me show you the frozen fish," said Jamie as he ran back with the ice block.

While Jamie was running, he accidentally stepped into a hole he had cut before. Jamie dropped his ice block onto the frozen lake and fell into the hole with a big splash.

"Help! It is too cold in the water," Jamie yelled as he kicked and struck the water.

"Hold on!" said Jack as he put down his fishing pole and ran towards Jamie. "I'm coming to rescue you!" Andrew also ran towards Jamie.

Jamie struggled hard in the water.

"It's freezing!" yelled Jamie. "Something is pulling my foot."

He looked into the water and saw a big fish pulling him. Jamie was dragged underwater, where he saw many fish swimming.

"Now I believe fish are alive under the ice," Jamie shouted while trying to stay afloat.

Jamie was pulled back into the water by the big fish. He tried to catch the tail of the fish, but the fish was very slippery. Jamie held the body of the big fish tightly and the fish struggled to swim away.

"我拿冻鱼给你看看。"杰米说着,拿着冰块往回跑。

他跑着跑着,突然踩进了他挖的一个洞。他的冰块掉在冰面上。杰米掉到洞里,水溅了出来。

"救命啊!救命啊!"杰米大叫。"水太冷啦!"

"别着急!"捷克说着,放下钓鱼竿向杰米跑去,"我来救你啦!"安德烈也向杰米跑去。

杰米在水中拼命挣扎。

"我快冻死啦!"杰米大叫,"有什么东西在拖我的脚。"

杰米向下看,发现一条大鱼正在拉扯他。杰米被拉到水下。他看到很多鱼在水中游来游去。

"现在我相信鱼在冰下面仍然活着。"杰米喊着,试图浮上来。

"Jamie! Jamie! Where are you? I cannot see you," Jack shouted into the hole.

Suddenly, Jamie felt himself rise from the water. He still held the fish tightly and felt the fish moving upward.

"I caught a big fish!" Jamie heard Andrew's voice. "Jack, come to help me."

Jack ran back to help Andrew. Jack and Andrew pulled the fishing pole together and dragged the fish out of water. They were amazed to see that Jamie was holding the fish, out of water.

"Jamie! You are saved," Jack exclaimed happily.

"Jamie, I thought you were a big fish!" said Andrew.

杰米再次被鱼拉到水下。杰米试图抓住大鱼的尾巴，可是大鱼很滑。杰米紧紧抱住鱼身，鱼使劲挣扎，游得很快。

"杰米！杰米！你在哪里？我看不见你！"捷克对洞里喊。

杰米突然看到前面有亮光。他紧紧抱住鱼，感到大鱼在向上移动。

"我钓到了一条大鱼。"杰米听到安德烈的声音。

捷克跑回去帮助安德烈。他和安德烈一起拉钓竿，把鱼拖出水。他们惊奇地发现，杰米抱着鱼出了水。

"杰米！你得救了。"捷克高兴地感叹。

"杰米，我还以为你是一条大鱼呢！"安德烈说。

"我们回家吧，"捷克说，"这样杰米就不会被冻坏啦。"

捷克脱下自己的外套，把杰米紧紧包住。安德烈把鱼放回水里。他们拿了工具，跑回家。

"Let's go home so Jamie won't get frozen," said Jack.

Jack took off his own jacket and wrapped it around Jamie. Andrew released the fish back into water. They took their tools and ran back home.

Jamie took a hot shower.

"I feel much warmer now," said Jamie. "I really saw fish swimming under the ice. I just wonder why they are not frozen."

"Normally, the density of a liquid is lower than the density of its solid state," said Jack. "Is that right?"

"Yes," said Jamie and Andrew.

"When water is frozen, it becomes solid ice," said Jack. "However, the density of ice is lower than the density of water."

"I see!" said Jamie. "That explains why ice floats on water."

"Yes!" said Jack. "If ice were denser than water, ice would sink to the bottom of the lake. Then the whole lake would freeze and all the fish would be frozen inside."

"I see," said Jamie. "So actually the ice will float on the water. The fish will be happily swimming in the water under the ice."

"Yes," said Jack.

杰米洗了个热水澡。

"我感觉暖和多了,"杰米说,"我真的看到鱼在冰下游泳。我不知道为什么他们没被冻住。"

"通常情况下,液体的密度比固体的低。"捷克说,"对吧?"

"是!"杰米和安德烈说。

"当水被冻结,就成了冰。"捷克说,"可是,冰的密度小于水。"

"我明白了!"杰米说,"这就能解释为什么冰会浮在水上了。"

"是啊!"捷克说,"假如冰密度比水的大,冰就会沉下去。整个湖都会冻住。然后所有的鱼都会被冻死在里面。"

"我懂了!"杰米说,"所以冰浮在水面上,鱼就可以高兴地在冰下的水里游泳。"

"是!"捷克说。

"上帝考虑得真周到啊!"杰米和安德烈喊着说。

"God is very considerate!" shouted Jamie and Andrew.

"Praise the Lord," said Jack. "From this phenomenon, we can understand that God takes care of the fish He creates. He won't allow them to become frozen fish in the winter."

"Thank God!" said Jamie. "I did not become a frozen mouse when I fell into the water."

"赞美主！"捷克说,"从这一现象,我们可以明白,上帝看顾祂所创造的鱼。祂不会让他们成为冬天的冻鱼。"

"感谢上帝！"杰米说,"我掉到水里,也没有成为冻鼠。"

Discussion Questions and Activities:

1. What did Jamie expect about ice fishing?
2. Did Jamie find many fish in the ice when he dug out an ice block?
3. Why did Jamie find one fish in an ice block?
4. What did Jamie observe when he fell into water?
5. Memorize Matthew 6:26, "Look at the birds of the air: they neither sow nor reap nor gather into barns, and yet your heavenly Father feeds them. Are you not of more value than they?"
6. Do a simple experiment. Put ice into water and observe if the ice floats or sinks.
7. How come the fish in the lake won't be frozen to death in winter?
8. What can we tell about God's love from this story?
9. With the help of parents, go ice fishing at a lake in winter.

杰米传奇（第二卷）

讨论问题和活动：

1. 杰米对冰钓有什么期待？
2. 杰米挖出一个冰块的时候，在冰里找到许多鱼吗？
3. 为什么杰米在一个冰块里找到一条鱼？
4. 杰米掉到水里，观察到什么？
5. 请背诵《马太福音》6:26："你们看那天上的飞鸟，也不种、也不收、也不积蓄在仓里，你们的天父尚且养活它。你们不比飞鸟贵重得多么？"
6. 做一个简单的实验：把冰块放入水中，观察冰是会漂浮还是下沉。
7. 为什么湖里的鱼在冬天不会被冻死？
8. 我们从这个故事中怎样看到上帝的爱？
9. 在成人的帮助下，冬天到湖上冰钓。

7. CAN JAMIE FIX EVERYTHING WITH DUCT TAPE?

"I am the most handy mouse in the world," said the little white mouse Jamie. "I can fix everything."

"Yes! You can fix everything," said the little gray mouse Andrew, laughing. "However, you fix everything with duct tape."

"What's wrong with using duct tape?" asked Jamie. "It works! I discovered that duct tape is the most useful tool in the world. It's the only tool in the world that can fix everything."

7. 杰米能用胶带修好一切吗？

"我是世界上手最巧的老鼠，"小白鼠杰米说，"我可以修好一切东西。"

"是！你是可以修好一切东西，"小灰鼠安德烈说，"不过，你用胶带来修好一切东西。"安德烈笑了起来。

"用胶带有什么错？"杰米说，"它很好用！我发现胶带是世界上最有用的工具。它是世界上唯一可以修复一切的工具。"

"Yes! It works," said Andrew. "However, it only works for a little while."

"What's wrong with a little while?" asked Jamie. "Our lives are just a little while long. Who cares about a longer time?"

"No," said Andrew. "We cannot just think about a short period of time. We have to think about a long period of time, even eternal life."

"I don't want to argue with you," said Jamie. "I will show you my skills. Let's go to my room."

Andrew followed Jamie into Jamie's room.

"Wow," Andrew said, his eyes widening and jaw dropping. "You fixed everything with duct tape!"

"Yes!" Jamie said with a smile. "The magical duct tape."

"是！它是很好用，"安德烈说，"不过，它只能适用一小会儿。"

"一小会儿有什么错？"杰米说，"我们的生命就只是一小会儿那么短。谁会在乎长期呢？"

"不，"安德烈说，"我们不能只考虑短期。我们要考虑长期，甚至永恒的生命。"

"我不想跟你争论，"杰米说，"我会让你看看我的技能。去我的房间看看。"

安德烈跟着杰米走进杰米的房间。

"哇，"安德烈的嘴巴和眼睛张得老大，"你用胶带来修所有东西！"

"是啊！"杰米说着，面带微笑。"神奇的胶带。"

"你打破的相框，"安德烈说，"你的破杯子，铅笔盒，笔，蜡笔，书的封面，椅子腿，裂开的窗玻璃，甚至破床单都用胶带来修。"

"现在你知道我神奇的技能了吧，"杰米说。

"你的杯子可能会漏水，"安德烈说。

"Your cracked photo frame," said Andrew, pointing to a photograph. "Your broken mug, pencil box, pens, crayons, torn book covers, broken chair legs, broken window and even your ripped blanket were fixed with duct tape."

"Now you know my magical skill," said Jamie.

"Your mug may leak," said Andrew.

"It leaks a little bit," said Jamie. "It doesn't matter too much. Don't you remember the saying, 'don't cry over spilled tea'?"

"Spilled milk, I think," said Andrew. "The duct tape makes your window look ugly. The duct tape even blocks part of your photo in your photo frame."

"They don't have to look beautiful," said Jamie. "The most important thing is that they can work."

Jack came into the room and said, "Do you mice want to play baseball?"

"That's a great idea!" said Jamie. "I love playing baseball. Jamie, the greatest mouse baseball player in the world."

"I also want to go," said Andrew. "I can be the umpire."

"I will be the pitcher then," said Jack. "Let's take our baseball gears with us."

"Let me get them, "said Andrew. "I'll get the baseball, gloves, bats and helmets."

"会漏一点儿,"杰米说,"没大关系。你不记得俗语说:'不要对着打翻的茶哭'吗?"

"我认为原话是'打翻的牛奶',"安德烈说,"胶带让你的窗户很难看。胶带甚至把你相框里的照片挡住了一部分。"

"它们不用看上去那么美,"杰米说,"最重要的是它们能用。"

捷克走了进来,说:"你们想去打棒球吗?"

"好主意!"杰米说,"我爱打棒球。我,杰米,是世界上最伟大的老鼠击球手。"

"我也很想去,"安德烈说,"我可以做接球手。"

"那我可以做投球手,"捷克说,"让我们带上打球用具吧。"

"我去拿,"安德烈说,"我会拿上棒球手套、球棒和头盔。"

"Let me get my duct tape," said Jamie. "I take my duct tape with me wherever I go. Don't forget, it's the most useful tool in the world."

Andrew shook his head.

The three friends walked to the baseball field close to their house.

Jamie stood at the home position of the baseball diamond and hit the ground with his baseball bat three times to show he was ready.

Jack threw the baseball, and Jamie hit it far away. Andrew ran to get the ball. Jamie dropped his bat and started running the bases.

Jamie ran back to the home plate before Andrew threw the baseball back to Jack.

"I won," Jamie said, jumping up and down. "I got one point."

Jamie picked up his baseball bat. He saw that half the bat was bent.

"Oops," said Jamie. "My baseball bat is cracked."

"Let me see," said Andrew.

Andrew took the bat and bent it even more, snapping it into two pieces.

"Sorry, Jamie," said Andrew. "I didn't break it on purpose."

"This is a beginner's plastic baseball bat," said Jack. "It can break easily."

"我去拿我的胶带,"杰米说,"无论我走到哪里,我都带着我的胶带。不要忘记,它是世界上最有用的工具。"

安德烈摇摇头。

三个朋友走到家附近的棒球场。

杰米站在棒球场的本垒的位置,用他的球棒打地面三次,以表示他已经准备好。

安德烈投棒球。杰米将球打得老远。安德烈跑去捡球。杰米扔下球棒,做本垒打。

安德烈把球扔回给捷克以先,杰米已经跑回本垒。

"我赢了,"杰米上蹦下跳,"我得到了一分啦。"

杰米捡起他的球棒。看到球棒弯了一半。

"哎呀,"杰米说,"我的球棒裂开了。"

"让我看看,"安德烈说。

安德烈拿着球棒一弯。球棒断成两截。

"对不起,杰米,"安德烈说,"我不是故意把球棒折断的。"

"Don't worry," said Jamie. "I can fix it with my duct tape."

"Jamie, you don't need to fix it," said Jack. "We can buy a new one for you."

"Let me show you," said Jamie. "The bat will work again." Jamie taped the two pieces together with his duct tape, "Look, I've fixed it."

"I don't think the bat will be strong enough," said Andrew. "It won't last very long."

"This bat will last forever," said Jamie. "Let's go on with our game. I will show you. I've made a baseball bat that works like a new one."

Andrew and Jack went back to their positions and got ready.

Jamie hit the ground with his bat three times.

Andrew pitched the ball. Jamie hit the ball with his bat. The bat immediately bent into a right angle.

Andrew laughed and said, "Your bat cannot even work with one hit."

"I can fix it with more duct tape," said Jamie.

Jamie put the bat on the ground and stepped on the bat to straighten it.

"Do you fix your bat this way?" Andrew said while shaking his head.

Jamie picked up the bat and wrapped it with more duct tape. He wrapped the bat with fifty

"这是一个初学者用的塑料球棒，"捷克说，"它很容易折断。"

"别担心，"杰米说，"我可以用胶带把它修好。"

"杰米，你不用修啦，"捷克说，"我们可以给你买根新球棒。"

"让我修好给你看看，"杰米说，"它会再次能用。"杰米用胶带把两段粘在一起，"看，我把它修好啦。"

"我觉得球棒强度不够，"安德烈说，"它用不了多久。"

"它能永远用下去，"杰米说，"我们继续打球。我会让你看到。我修好的球棒会象新的一样好用。"

安德烈和捷克回到了自己的位置准备好了。杰米用球棒敲地面三次。安德烈投球。杰米用球棒击球。球棒立即弯曲成了直角。

"哈哈，"安德烈笑了，"你的球棒受不了一击。"

circles of tape, which formed a ball in the middle of the bat.

"Now you have a baseball in the middle of your bat," said Andrew, laughing.

"Just pitch the ball," said Jamie. "The bat will surely work this time."

"Let's go on with our game," said Jack.

Andrew pitched the baseball. Jamie hit the

ball with his baseball bat. The bat broke and half of the bat flew away.

Jamie threw the rest of the bat to the ground and cried.

"Don't cry, Jamie," Jack said while hugging Jamie. "We can buy a new bat for you."

"But I still think I can fix things with my duct tape," said Jamie while he wiped his tears.

"Jamie, if something does not last eternally," said Jack, "it will perish quite soon."

"我可以用更多的胶带来修好它，"杰米说。

杰米把球棒放在地上，把球棒踩直。

"你这样修复你的球棒吗？"安德烈摇着头。

杰米拿起球棒，用更多胶带来包裹。他包裹了50圈的胶带，在棒中间形成一个球。

"现在你的球棒中间有个棒球啦，"安德烈笑了起来。

"投球吧，"杰米说，"球棒这次一定能用。"

"我们继续打球吧，"捷克说。

安德烈投棒球。杰米用球棒击中了球。球棒折断，一半飞走了。杰米把剩下的一半球棒扔在地上，哭了起来。

"别哭了，杰米，"捷克拥抱杰米，"我们可以为你买一根新的球棒。"

"但我还是认为我可以用胶带修好东西，"杰米说着，一面擦着眼泪。

One week later, Jamie and Andrew went to volunteer in Jack's class at Happy Hollow School. They were going to do a scientific magic show using batteries.

Andrew and Jamie set up the experiments. The students and the teacher were watching.

"Oops!" said Andrew. "I forgot the clips for attaching the wires to the battery poles. We cannot do this experiment anymore."

"Don't worry," said Jamie while he took out his duct tape. "I always have my duct tape with me. We can fix it using duct tape."

"That looks like a choice when we don't have any other choices," said Andrew.

Jamie taped the wires to the poles of the battery.

"Your duct tape works!" said Andrew. "Jamie, you've really fixed it."

"Duct tape does not work with everything," Jamie said with a smile. "However, for this temporary experiment, it can work. We should still use clips next time."

"杰米，如果一件东西没有永恒价值，"捷克说，"它很快就会消亡。"

一个星期后，杰米和安德烈来到捷克的快乐谷小学做志愿者。他们要用电池做科学魔术表演。安德烈和杰米在安装实验用具。学生和教师在观看。

"糟糕！"安德烈说，"我忘了带把电线接到电池两极的夹子啦。我们做不了这个实验啦。"

"别担心，"杰米说着，一面掏出胶带，"我随时携带我的胶带。我们可以用胶带来修好它。"

"这是没有办法的办法啦，"安德烈说。

杰米用胶带把电线贴到电池的两极。

"你的胶带很有用！"安德烈说，"杰米，你真的把它修好啦。"

"胶带不能解决一切问题，"杰米说，面带微笑，"不过，对这样临时的工作，它可以有用。我们下一次还是应该用夹子。"

Discussion Questions and Activities:

1. How did Jamie fix everything?
2. Do you think it's a good idea to fix everything with duct tape?
3. How did Jamie fix the broken baseball bat for the first time?
4. Did the bat work?
5. How did Jamie fix the baseball bat the second time?
6. Did the bat work this time?
7. How did the duct tape help in their scientific magic show?
8. With the help of your parents, use duct tape to fix something broken.
9. Memorize 1 John 2:17, "And the world is passing away along with its desires, but whoever does the will of God abides forever."

杰米传奇（第二卷）

讨论问题和活动：

1. 杰米是怎样修好一切东西的？
2. 你认为用胶带来修复一切是个好主意吗？
3. 杰米第一次是怎样修复打破的球棒？球棒能用吗？
4. 杰米第二次怎样修复球棒呢？这次球棒能用吗？
5. 胶带怎样帮助了杰米和安德烈的科学魔术表演？
6. 在父母的帮助下，用胶带修好一件打破的东西。
7. 请背诵经文《约翰一书》2:17 "这世界、和其上的情欲，都要过去。惟独遵行神旨意的，是永远常存。"

8. DOES THE TOOTH FAIRY EXIST??

"I lost a tooth," Jack said at the dining table. He showed his tooth to the whole family and opened his mouth wide. "Look at this hole. I'm going to put this tooth under my pillow tonight. I think the tooth fairy will take it and leave one dollar under my pillow."

"How did you lose your tooth?" asked Dr. Charlie.

"Jack played basketball with Andrew and me this afternoon," said the little white mouse Jamie, "The ball hit his mouth and knocked a tooth out."

8. 牙仙存在吗？

"我掉了一颗牙，"捷克在餐桌上向全家宣布。他把牙齿给全家看，还把嘴张得大大的，"看这个洞。我今晚要把牙齿放在我的枕头下。我想牙仙会把牙齿拿去，然后在我枕头下面放一块钱。"

"你的牙齿是怎么掉的？"查理博士问。

"This is my eleventh tooth that fell out," said Jack, "I have already got ten dollars from the tooth fairy."

"That sounds like an easy way to make money," said Jamie, "I wish my teeth could also fall out so I can get money. However, my teeth can never fall out."

"We are rodents," said the little gray mouse Andrew, "Our teeth never fall out. They just keep growing, so we need to grind our teeth all the

"今天下午捷克、安德烈和我在一起打篮球,"小白鼠杰米说,"球击中他的嘴,把他的牙齿撞了下来。"

"这是我掉的第 11 颗牙齿,"捷克说,"我已经从牙仙得到了十块钱。"

"这听起来像一个快速赚钱的方法,"杰米说,"我希望我的牙齿也会脱落,这样我就可以拿到钱了。可惜,我的牙齿从不会脱落。"

"我们是啮齿类动物,"小灰鼠安德烈说,"我们的牙齿从不会脱落。它们只是一直长,所以我们需要经常磨牙。"安德烈拿起一根筷子来磨牙。

第二天一早,大家都听到捷克在他的卧室里喊叫。

"一块钱!"捷克喊着,"昨晚牙仙来拿走了我的牙齿。"

杰米和安德烈冲进捷克的房间,看到捷克拿着一张一美元的钞票,在床上上蹦下跳。

time." Andrew started to grind his teeth on a chopstick.

Early next morning, everybody heard Jack shouting from his bedroom.

"One dollar!" Jack shouted, "The tooth fairy came last night and took my tooth."

Jamie and Andrew ran into Jack's room and saw Jack holding a one-dollar bill, jumping on his bed.

"I also want to get money from the tooth fairy," Jamie said to Andrew while they walked out of Jack's room. "Could you help me?"

"What can I do for you?" asked Andrew.

"Let me think," replied Jamie. "Maybe you can pull out one of my teeth using a pair of pliers."

Jamie and Andrew found Dr. Charlie's toolbox and Andrew took out a pair of pliers.

"Open your mouth really wide," said Andrew, "I am the world's best mouse dentist who can pull out a baby tooth, even for a mouse!" Andrew clamped one of Jamie's teeth and started to pull.

"Ouch!" said Jamie as he jumped away, "This is too painful!"

"You can't get your money if you're afraid of the pain," said Andrew as he ran towards Jamie.

"No! No! It's too painful!" said Jamie as he ran away from Andrew.

"我也想从牙仙得到钱,"杰米对安德烈说着,他们一面走出捷克的房间,"你能帮助我吗?"

"我怎样帮助你呀?"安德烈问道。

"让我想想,"杰米回答说,"也许你可以用一把钳子把我的牙齿拔下来。"

杰米和安德烈去查理博士的工具箱里找,安德烈找到一把钳子。

"把嘴大大张开,"安德烈说,"我是世界上最好的牙医老鼠,我可以拔乳牙,甚至是给老鼠拔牙!"安德烈夹住杰米的一颗牙齿,开始拔。

"哎呀!"杰米说着,跳了起来,"太疼啦!"

"如果你怕痛,就拿不到钱,"安德烈说着,向杰米跑来。

"不!不!太疼啦!"杰米说着,从安德烈身边跑开。

The two mice ran around the whole house. When Jamie tried to climb upstairs, his feet slipped. He lost his balance, and his mouth hit the handrail of the stairs. One of his teeth fell out.

"One of my teeth fell out! You did a great job, my best friend!" said Jamie while he picked up

his tooth.

Andrew stopped chasing Jamie and said, "Let me look at the tooth."

Jamie handed the tooth to Andrew.

"I told you I'm the best mouse dentist ever!" said Andrew as he observed the tooth carefully.

The next morning, the whole family was eating breakfast at their dining table.

杰米传奇（第二卷）

两只老鼠在整个房子里追逐。当杰米想爬到楼上，他脚下一滑。他失去平衡，嘴撞到楼梯扶手上。他的一颗牙齿掉了下来。

"我的牙齿掉下来了！你干得非常出色，我最好的朋友！"杰米说着，捡起他的牙齿。

安德烈停止追逐杰米，说，"嗯，让我看看这颗牙齿。"

杰米把牙齿递给安德烈。

"我告诉过你，我是有史以来最优秀的牙医老鼠！"安德烈说着，仔细观察牙齿。

第二天早上，全家人在餐桌旁吃早餐。

"杰米，你看上去很伤心，"安德烈说，"昨晚，牙仙有拿走你的牙齿，在枕头下面放一元钱吗？"

"我觉得牙仙不存在，"杰米说着，眼含泪水，"这只是一个童话。今天早晨，我的牙齿还在我的枕头下，没有钱。"

"可怜的杰米，也许昨晚牙仙收集牙齿太忙，"查理博士说，"今晚再把你的牙齿放在枕头下。我相信明天早上你一定会拿到钱的。"

"Jamie, you look very sad," said Andrew. "Did the tooth fairy take your tooth and have one dollar under your pillow last night?"

"I don't think the tooth fairy exists at all," said Jamie with tears in his eyes. "It is just a fairy tale. My tooth was still under my pillow this morning without any money."

"My poor little Jamie, maybe the tooth fairy was too busy with collecting teeth last night," said Dr. Charlie. "Put your tooth under your pillow again tonight. I believe you will surely get your money tomorrow morning."

"Okay," said Jamie. "I will try again tonight."

That night before Jamie went to bed, he told Andrew about his plan.

"That's a great idea!" said Andrew.

At midnight, the door to Jamie's bedroom opened. A black shadow came in and reached his hand under Jamie's pillow.

"The tooth fairy!" screamed the two mice.

"What happened?" shouted Jack as he ran into Jamie's bedroom. Anna and Sally were behind him.

The lights suddenly turned on. Andrew had turned on the light, while Jamie was holding a camera.

"Cheese, tooth fairy," said Jamie as he pressed down the shutter button on the camera.

"好吧，"杰米说。"今晚我会再试一次。"

那天晚上杰米上床睡觉前，他和安德烈谈起他的计划。

"这是一个奇妙的想法！"安德烈说。

午夜时分，杰米的卧室门开了。一个黑色的影子进来了，把手伸到杰米的枕头下。

"牙仙！"两只小老鼠尖叫。

灯光突然打开。安德烈打开灯。杰米拿着相机。

"怎么啦？"捷克喊着，跑进了杰米的卧室。安娜和莎莉在他身后。

"微笑，牙仙，"杰米说着，按下相机上的快门按钮。

"查理博士，你在这里做什么呀？"安德烈问道。

大家都看到了查理博士穿着睡衣在房间的中间。他的眼睛和嘴巴张得大大的。他左手拿着一美元，右手拿着杰米的牙齿。

"我来看看牙仙做了什么，"查理博士说。"你们两个老鼠吓了我一跳。"

"Dr. Charlie, what are you doing here?" asked Andrew.

Everybody saw Dr. Charlie standing in the middle of the room in his pajamas. His eyes and mouth were wide open. He was holding one dollar in his left hand. His right hand was holding Jamie's tooth.

"I'm here to see what the tooth fairy did," said Dr. Charlie. "The two of you scared me."

"Andrew, I told you that the tooth fairy doesn't exist," said Jamie. "The parents took the tooth and put one dollar under the pillow."

"I have been cheated," said Jack. "Why did you cheat on me, Daddy?"

"安德烈,我告诉过你,牙仙根本不存在,"杰米说,"父母把牙齿拿走,在枕头下面放一元钱。"

"我被欺骗了,"捷克说,"你为什么骗我,爸爸?"

安娜拿来一个小盒子,把它交给捷克,"你所有的十一颗乳牙都在这里,"她说。

捷克打开了盒子,说:"哇,它们看起来太可爱了!我都不记得我第一次掉的乳牙那么小。"

"孩子们,牙仙只是一个童话,"安娜说,"当孩子们掉乳牙的时候,这个故事鼓励他们要勇敢。将来,你会告诉你的孩子同样的故事。然而,《圣经》里所有的故事都是历史上真的发生过的。"

"爸爸,妈妈,谢谢你们的爱,"捷克说着,一面拥抱父母,"牙仙是否存在并不重要。最重要的是你们爱我。"

莎莉也拥抱了她的父母。

Anna brought a tiny box and gave it to Jack. "All your eleven baby teeth are here," she said.

Jack opened the box and said, "Wow, they look so cute! I can't even remember my first lost baby tooth to be so tiny."

"Kids, the tooth fairy is just a fairy tale," said Anna, "The story encourages kids to be brave when they lose a tooth. You will tell the same story to your kids in the future. However, all the stories in the Bible really happened historically. The New Testament books were written mostly by the Apostles who saw Jesus."

"Daddy, Mommy, thank you for your love," said Jack as he hugged his parents. "It's not important whether the tooth fairy exists or not. The most important thing is that you love me."

Sally also hugged her parents.

"Thank you for knocking out my tooth, the world's best dentist mouse," said Jamie as he hugged Andrew. "Love is the most important thing, even more important than the tooth fairy or the money."

"谢谢你敲掉我的牙齿,世界上最优秀的老鼠牙医,"杰米说着,拥抱安德烈,"爱是最重要的事情。它比牙仙或金钱更重要。"

Discussion Questions and Activities:

1. How did Jack lose his tooth?
2. Did Jack get the money?
3. Why won't Jamie and Andrew lose their teeth?
4. How did Andrew help Jamie to pull out a tooth?
5. Did Jamie get the money from the tooth fairy?
6. What happened in Jamie's room at midnight?
7. Does the tooth fairy exist?
8. What's the purpose of the tooth fairy story?
9. What's the difference between the Bible stories and the tooth fairy story?
10. What's more important than the money or the tooth fairy?
11. Memorize Psalm 96:5 "For all the gods of the peoples are worthless idols, but the Lord made the heavens."
12. Memorize 2 Peter 1:16, "We did not follow cleverly devised myths when we made known to you the power and coming of our Lord Jesus Christ, but we were eyewitnesses of his majesty."

杰米传奇（第二卷）

讨论问题和活动：

1. 捷克的牙齿是怎样掉的？
2. 捷克得到钱了吗？
3. 为什么杰米和安德烈不会掉牙齿？
4. 安德烈怎样帮助杰米拔牙？
5. 杰米从牙仙得到钱了吗？
6. 半夜在杰米的房间里发生了什么事？
7. 牙仙存在吗？
8. 牙仙传说的目的是什么？
9. 圣经故事和牙仙的童话故事之间的区别是什么？
10. 比金钱或牙仙更重要的是什么？
11. 请背诵经文《诗篇》96:5 "外邦的神都属虚无。惟独耶和华创造诸天。"
12. 请背诵经文《彼得后书》1:16 "我们从前，将我们主耶稣基督的大能、和他降临的事，告诉你们，并不是随从乖巧捏造的虚言，乃是亲眼见过他的威荣。"

9. CAN JAMIE SKY-DIVE WITHOUT A PARACHUTE?

"I feel very excited to go skydiving," said the little gray mouse Andrew. "This is my first time. I will glide like a bird in the sky."

"Yes," said Jack. "Don't forget your parachute."

"I don't need a parachute," said the little white mouse Jamie.

Jack, Sally, Andrew, and Jamie were in an airplane for skydiving. They were talking about their thrilling adventure.

"How come you don't need a parachute?" asked Jack.

9. 杰米不需要降落伞就能空降吗?

"我要跳伞啦!我太兴奋啦!"小灰鼠安德烈说,"这是我第一次跳伞。我会像小鸟一样在天空中滑翔。"

"是的,"捷克说,"不要忘记你的降落伞。"

"我才不需要降落伞呢,"小白鼠杰米说。

捷克,莎莉,杰米和安德烈乘坐飞机去跳伞。他们在谈论惊险刺激的探险。

"I'm the smartest mouse in the world," said Jamie, "I can glide without a parachute."

"That's dangerous," said Sally. "Nobody can skydive without a parachute."

"I'm not afraid," said Jamie. "I can rely on my own power. I'm a super mouse."

"You will drop like a rock," said Andrew. "You will punch a six-foot deep hole in the ground."

"I can wear a helmet then," said Jamie while he held up his helmet.

"Then you will punch an eight-foot deep hole," said Andrew.

"Jamie," said Jack, "you just cannot rely on yourself. A parachute can save your life."

"Okay, okay," said Jamie. "I will use the parachute this time. You lost the opportunity to see the gliding of the super mouse without a parachute."

An alarm sounded.

"Everybody, get ready to dive," shouted the captain.

Everybody, including Jamie, put their parachute bags on their backs and their helmets on.

The captain opened the side gate. A gust of strong wind blew into the plane.

"This is dangerous," said Jamie.

"Ready, jump," shouted the captain.

Jack jumped off the plane.

"为什么？"捷克问道。

"我是世界上最优秀的跳伞老鼠，"杰米说，"我不需要降落伞就可以滑翔。"

"这太危险啦，"莎莉说，"没有人能够不用降落伞就在天空滑翔。"

"我不怕，"杰米说，"我可以依靠自己的能力。我是一只超级老鼠。"

"你会象一块石头一样坠落，"安德烈说，"然后，在地上撞一个六英尺深的洞。"

"我可以戴上头盔，"杰米说着，拿起他的头盔。

"这样你会撞一个八英尺深的洞，"安德烈说。

"杰米，"捷克说，"你不能靠自己。降落伞可以救你的命。"

"好啦，好啦，"杰米说，"我这次就用降落伞吧。你失去了观看超级老鼠不用降落伞就滑翔的机会。"

警报响起。

"准备跳伞，"机长喊道。

Jamie looked down and saw Jack's parachute opened a little while after Jack jumped off.

Next, Sally also jumped.

"Jamie, never jump without a parachute," Andrew said to Jamie, and then Andrew jumped off.

It was Jamie's turn to jump.

Jamie walked to the gate, and looked down. He saw three parachutes flying in the sky like three flowers. Jamie looked down, and everything looked so tiny. The houses looked like matchboxes. The cars looked like tiny bugs.

"This is scary," said Jamie.

"Do you want to jump now?" asked the captain.

大家背上自己的降落伞包，戴上头盔，包括杰米。

机长打开侧门。一阵大风刮进了飞机。

"这太危险啦，"杰米说。

"预备，跳，"机长说。

捷克跳下飞机。

杰米向下看，看到捷克跳出去以后，很快降落伞打开。

接下来，莎莉也跳了下去。

"杰米，决不要不带降落伞就跳，"安德烈对杰米说，然后安德烈跳了下去。

轮到杰米跳了。

杰米到门前，向下看。他看到了三朵降落伞在天空上滑翔，好像三朵盛开的鲜花。杰米看着地面，一切都显得如此的渺小。房子看上去像火柴盒。汽车看起来像小虫。

"真吓人，"杰米说。

"你现在想跳吗？"机长问。

"让我想想，"杰米说，"我真的很害怕呀！"

"Let me think," said Jamie. "I am really scared." Jamie's legs trembled.

A gust of strong wind blew over. Jamie lost his balance and fell out of the gate.

"Help!" yelled Jamie.

He heard the captain saying, "I know you can make it." Then he heard the captain closing the door.

Jamie fell down like a rock.

"Help!" said Jamie. "I don't want to die."

"Just pull the rope on your shoulder," shouted Jack.

Jamie tried to pull the rope on his shoulder to open his parachute. However, the parachute could not open.

"Help me!" screamed Jamie. "I don't want to punch a deep hole into the ground."

Jamie kept falling down. He closed his eyes.

Suddenly he fell onto a piece of cloth. Jamie opened his eyes and found he fell onto Andrew's white parachute.

"I'm still alive," shouted Jamie. "I'm still alive! Look, I can glide without a parachute."

"Great job," shouted Jack.

"I told you I'm a super mouse," shouted Jamie while he was dancing on Andrew's parachute. The parachute was big, just like a big stage for Jamie.

杰米的腿在打颤。

一股强风吹过来。杰米失去了平衡,从门口跌了下去。

"救命啊!"杰米大叫。

他听到机长说,"我知道你能做到"。然后,他听到机长关上了门。

杰米像一块石头一样坠落。

"救命啊!"杰米说,"我不想死啊。"

"拉你肩膀上的绳子来打开降落伞,"捷克喊道。

杰米试图拉他的肩膀上的绳子。然而,降落伞无法打开。

"救命啊!"杰米尖叫,"我不想在地上撞一个洞。"

杰米不停往下坠落。他闭上了眼睛。

他突然掉到一块布上。杰米睁开眼睛,发现他掉到安德烈的白色降落伞面上。

"我还活着!"杰米喝道,"我还活着!看哪,我没有降落伞也可以滑翔。"

"做得好!"捷克喊道。

A gust of wind blew over Jamie. Jamie lost his balance and fell down and he slid down the parachute.

"Help!" said Jamie.

He slid off Andrew's parachute and dropped into the sky.

"I will punch a deep hole this time," screamed Jamie while he closed his eyes.

"Jamie, I'm coming," shouted Sally.

Sally controlled her red parachute to move over.

Jamie fell onto Sally's parachute.

"I didn't die," shouted Jamie while he opened his eyes. "I didn't die! This is really a miracle. Thank you, Sally."

"Hold on to the parachute," shouted Sally. "Don't dance on it anymore."

"Sure! Sure!" said Jamie. "Now I really understand I cannot rely on myself."

Jamie sat down and held the parachute cloth with his hands. He looked up and saw clouds in the blue sky. He looked around and saw Andrew's white parachute and Jack's yellow parachute gliding in the sky. When Jamie looked down, the houses, cars and rivers looked very tiny.

"This looks so beautiful," said Jamie. "When I sit high enough, I see such beautiful scenes."

"我告诉过你,我是一只超级老鼠,"杰米喊道,在安德烈的降落伞上跳舞。降落伞很大,就像一个大舞台。

一阵风吹到杰米。杰米失去平衡,摔倒了。他滑下降落伞面。

"救命啊!"杰米尖叫着。

他滑出安德烈的降落伞,在天空中下坠。

"这次,我会在地上撞一个大洞了,"杰米大叫,闭上了眼睛。

"杰米,我来了,"莎莉喊道。

莎莉控制她的红色降落伞移了过来。

杰米掉在莎莉的降落伞面上。

"我没死,"杰米喊着,睁开了眼睛,"我没死!这的确是一个奇迹。谢谢你,莎莉。"

"抓住降落伞布,"莎莉高呼,"不要再跳舞了。"

"一定!一定!"杰米说。"现在我才真正明白我不能靠自己。"

杰米坐了下来,用双手抓住降落伞布。他抬起头来看到蓝天飘着白云。他环顾四周,安

A black shadow moved fast towards Jamie.

Jamie looked upward and saw that an eagle was flying towards him.

"An eagle," screamed Jamie. "It's diving towards me. Help!"

"What should we do now?" shouted Andrew.

"I don't know," shouted Jack.

The eagle dived towards Jamie. Jamie ran around on the parachute. The eagle chased him tightly.

The eagle opened its talons and tried to catch Jamie.

As Jamie bent down, the eagle caught his helmet and flew past him.

德烈的白色降落伞和捷克的黄色降落伞在天空滑翔。杰米向下看，房子、汽车和河流显得非常微小。

"这看起来太美丽了，"杰米说，"当我坐得足够高时，我就可以看到这样美丽的风景。"

一个黑影在降落伞上向着杰米快速移动。

杰米向上一看，看到一只老鹰向他飞来。

"老鹰，"杰米大叫，"老鹰向我飞来啦！救命啊！"

"杰米，我们现在怎么帮你呀？"安德烈高呼。

"我不知道，"捷克喊道。

老鹰对着杰米俯冲。杰米在降落伞面上到处跑。老鹰紧紧追逐着他。

老鹰张开了爪子，想抓住杰米。

杰米一低身，老鹰抓住了他的头盔飞了过去。

"我的头盔！"杰米喊道，双手抱头，不停地跑。

"My helmet!" shouted Jamie while he put his hands on his head and kept running.

The eagle dropped the helmet, made a turn and flew back towards Jamie.

"No! No!" screamed Jamie and ran around.

The eagle's talons reached Jamie.

Jamie quickly ducked again.

The eagle grabbed the rope on Jamie's parachute.

The parachute immediately opened and the strong breeze pulled Jamie away.

The eagle didn't understand why Jamie suddenly disappeared, so it flew away.

Meanwhile, Jamie was gliding on his green parachute.

"I am gliding with my own parachute now," said Jamie. "I feel wonderful. My life is saved. I beat the eagle."

"Jamie," shouted Sally, "you're our great hero."

"Great job," shouted Jack.

"Jamie," shouted Andrew, "we feel happy for you."

Finally, the four friends landed in the airport.

"Hooray," said Jamie. "I landed on the ground without punching an eight-feet deep hole."

"You made it, Jamie," said Andrew.

"Jamie, you almost scared me to death," said Sally.

老鹰扔下头盔，转身向杰米飞去。

"不！不！"杰米尖叫着到处跑。

老鹰的爪子够到杰米。

杰米很快弯下身子。

老鹰抓住杰米的降落伞拉绳。

降落伞立刻打开，强大的力量把杰米拉得飞走。

老鹰不明白为什么杰米突然消失，就飞走了。

杰米乘着他的绿色降落伞滑翔。

"我现在用自己的降落伞滑翔啦，"杰米说，"我感觉太好啦。我的命得救啦。我击败了老鹰。"

"杰米，"莎莉喊道，"你是个大英雄。"

"杰米，"捷克说，"了不起！"

"杰米，"安德烈说，"我们为你感到高兴。"

最后，四个朋友在机场降落。

"太棒了，"杰米说，"我回到了地面，没有在地上撞一个八英尺深的洞。"

"Jamie," said Jack, "you're our hero. You handled such difficult situations."

"Do you know what I was doing when I was falling down?" asked Jamie.

"You were thinking about punching an eight-foot hole in a baseball field or a four-foot hole on a highway, I think," said Andrew.

"You were thinking about how you can fly in heaven," said Sally.

"You were thinking about getting two wings on your back," said Jack.

"I was praying to Jesus Christ," said Jamie. "Jesus is just like the parachute for my life. Without Him, my life will be like jumping off a plane without a parachute."

"Hallelujah!" applauded Sally, Jack and Andrew.

"你成功了，杰米，"安德烈说。

"杰米，你差点把我吓死了，"莎莉说。

"杰米，"捷克说，"你真是我们的英雄。你处理了这些困难的情况。"

"你知道我往下掉的时候我在做什么吗？"杰米问道。

"我想，你在考虑是在棒球场上撞个八英尺深的洞，还是在高速公路上撞一个四英尺深的洞。"安德烈说。

"你在想怎样飞上天堂，"莎莉说。

"你在希望背上长两个翅膀，"捷克说。

"我在向耶稣基督祈祷，"杰米说，"他就像是我生命中的降落伞。没有他，我的生命就会像不背降落伞从飞机上跳下一样。"

"哈利路亚！"莎莉，捷克和安德烈欢呼。

Discussion Questions and Activities:

1. Why did Jamie want to jump from an airplane without a parachute?
2. What happened to Jamie's parachute?
3. Why did Jamie fall of Andrew's parachute?
4. Why did the eagle fly away from Jamie?
5. Memorize 2 Thessalonians 3:3, "But the Lord is faithful. He will establish you and guard you against the evil one."
6. Watch a skydiving show with your parents, or borrow a skydiving video from your library.

杰米传奇（第二卷）

讨论问题和活动：

1. 为什么杰米想不背降落伞就跳下飞机？
2. 杰米的降落伞发生了什么事？
3. 为什么杰米从安德烈的降落伞上掉了下来？
4. 为什么老鹰从杰米身边飞走了？
5. 请背诵经文《帖撒罗尼迦后书》3:3，"但主是信实的，要坚固你们，保护你们脱离那恶者。"
6. 与你的父母一起观看跳伞表演，或从图书馆借跳伞的影片来观看。

10. CAN JAMIE WALK IN THE FIRE?

"Praise be to the God of Shadrach, Meshach and Abednego, who has sent his angel and rescued his servants!" Jack was reading Chapter 3 of the book of Daniel to Jamie and Andrew.

"The three friends of Daniel were big heroes," said the little gray mouse Andrew.

"I want to be a hero like them," said the little white mouse Jamie. "And it seems a big hero should always show up from the fire, with triumphant music around him, just like in the movies."

10. 杰米能在火里行走吗？

"沙得拉、米煞、亚伯尼歌的神，是应当称颂的。他差遣使者救护倚靠他的仆人！"捷克向杰米和安德烈阅读《但以理书》第3章。

"但以理的三个朋友真是大英雄啊。"安德烈说。

"我想成为像他们一样的英雄，"杰米说，"看来大英雄应该从火中显现，被胜利的音乐围绕，就像在电影里一样。"

"I will walk out of the fire step by step with music in the background. People will throw flowers to me, shouting, 'Our hero! Jamie, the greatest hero mouse in the world!' And they will applaud," Jamie was talking about his dream.

"Andrew, do you think I should run into fire as a scientific experiment?" Jamie asked Andrew.

"No way! You would become a barbecued mouse," said Andrew.

"I can pray to God sincerely when I am in the fire. God will protect me. I think my faith is strong enough," Jamie said.

"Jamie, God protected Daniel's friends before the king of Babylon," said Andrew. "God did not tell you, Jamie the mouse, to go into the fire, whether or not you pray hard. The Bible said, 'Do not put the Lord your God to the test'."

"I will show you that I can do it. This is a scientific experiment," Jamie said.

Jamie thought all day long about becoming a big hero walking out of the fire.

One week later, there came the opportunity.

It was a cold winter day. Dr. Charlie decided to light up burning wood in the fireplace.

Jack, Jamie, and Andrew helped to carry the logs.

Dr. Charlie put the logs into the fireplace and lit them. The wood started burning. Light and

"也许是吧,"安德烈说。

杰米谈到他的梦想:"我会随着背景音乐一步一步从火里走出。人们会在我面前鼓掌。人们会向我扔鲜花。人们会欢呼:'我们的英雄!杰米,世界上最伟大的英雄老鼠!'"

"安德烈,你觉得我应该试试跑到火里去做个科学实验吗?"杰米问安德烈。

"不行!你会成为烤老鼠肉的。"安德烈说。

"当我在火里时,我可以向上帝真诚祈祷。上帝会保护我的。我觉得我的信心足够大啦。"杰米说。

"杰米,上帝在巴比伦国王面前保护了但以理的的朋友,"捷克说。"上帝没有告诉你,杰米老鼠,跑到火里,不管你祈祷没有。圣经说:'不可试探主你的神。'"

"我会让你们看到,我能做到。这是一个科学实验。"杰米说。

杰米整天想着成为一个从火里走出来的大英雄。

the smell of wood came out of the fireplace. Half an hour later, all the logs turned into red coals.

Jamie had already prayed for half an hour, saying, "God bless me! God bless me! God bless me!..."

"I'm going into the fire! I want to be a hero like Daniel's friends! I'm sure God will protect

me!" Jamie shouted, and ran into the fireplace.

Dr. Charlie, Jack, and Andrew were astonished.

"Jamie, come out!" yelled Jack.

"My friend, you will be barbequed," Andrew cried while covering his eyes with his hands.

Jamie was running a half circle inside the fireplace.

一个星期后,机会来了。

这是冬天寒冷的一天。查理博士决定点着燃木壁炉。

捷克,杰米和安德烈帮助搬木头。

查理博士把木头放到壁炉里,点燃木头。木头开始燃烧。火光从壁炉里出来。大家闻到木头的气味。半小时后,所有的木头都变成了红色。

杰米已经祷告半小时:"上帝保佑我!上帝保佑我!上帝保佑我…"

"我要到火里去!我想成为但以理的朋友那样的英雄!我相信上帝会保护我的!"杰米喊着跑进了壁炉。

查理博士、捷克和安德烈大吃一惊。

"杰米,出来!"捷克大喊。

"我的朋友,你会被烧焦的,"安德烈双手捂着眼睛,哭了起来。

杰米在壁炉内跑了半圈。

查理博士立刻从桌子上拿了一杯水。

Dr. Charlie immediately grabbed a glass of water from the table.

Seconds later, Jamie had already ran out of the fireplace. He did not look too bad, but his fur was burnt, which made him look like naked. His whiskers were burned as well, and his tail was still on fire.

Dr. Charlie dumped the whole glass of water onto Jamie's head. White smoke rose from Jamie's body. Jamie was wet all over his body. The fire on his tail went out.

Jamie looked up and down his own body.

"I am not injured! I am not injured!" Jamie clapped his hands and jumped up and down.

"You could have killed yourself, little mouse," Dr. Charlie said.

"This is crazy and dangerous," Jack said.

"I almost lost my best friend," Andrew said while wiping his tears.

"I am okay," said Jamie. "I kept praying to God when I was running through the fireplace."

"That is way too dangerous. A true hero would never behave this way," Dr. Charlie said.

Jamie cried, bursting into tears.

"I agree," said Jack. "Daniel's friends went into the fire to glorify God. What is your purpose, Jamie? To show off? If you had died, would that

杰米传奇（第二卷）

几秒钟后，杰米已经跑出了壁炉。他看起来还不太糟糕。他的毛被烧了，使他看上去像是光着身子。他的胡须被烧了。他的尾巴在燃烧。

查理博士把整杯水倒在杰米头上。一股白色的烟雾从杰米身上冒起来。杰米全身都湿透了。他尾巴上的火熄灭了。

杰米上下打量着自己的身体。

"我没有受伤！我没有受伤！"杰米拍着手，上蹦下跳。

"你差点把自己害死了，小老鼠。"查理博士说。

"这太疯狂，太危险啦。"捷克说。

"我差点儿失去了我最好的朋友。"安德烈擦着眼泪。

"我没事。"杰米说："我在壁炉里跑的时候，我在不停地向上帝祈祷。"

"这太鲁莽了。一个真正的英雄决不会这样做。"查理博士说。

杰米哭了，泪水从眼眶里涌出来。

have any value? A barbequed mouse as a delicious meal for a cat?"

"Poor silly mouse," Andrew said.

Jamie cried even louder.

Several months later, Jamie's fur and whiskers grew back.

One Saturday morning, Sally, Jack, Andrew, and Jamie went to the town fire station for the Touch-a-Truck activity.

Jamie was very excited to climb up and down on the fire trucks. He also tried on the firefighter's uniform, boots, and hat. Of course, the smallest size. Jack took pictures for Jamie when Jamie was sitting on a fire truck with his uniforms on.

"May I become a firefighter?" Jamie asked the firefighter chief.

"Of course, when you grow up!" said the firefighter chief.

Suddenly, an alarm went off.

All the firefighters jumped onto the fire trucks and the fire trucks rushed out of the station.

Jamie was still on a fire truck, wearing the firefighter uniform, boots and hat. When Jack pressed down the shutter button on his camera, he found that Jamie was not in the picture.

"我同意,"捷克说,"但以理的朋友投入火中去荣耀神。杰米,你的目的是什么呢?炫耀自己吗?如果你死了,那有任何价值吗?成了一个烧烤老鼠作猫的美餐?"

"可怜的傻老鼠。"安德烈说。

杰米哭得更响了。

两个月后,杰米的毛和胡须长了回来。

一个星期六,莎莉,捷克,安德烈和杰米去镇消防站的开放日。

杰米兴奋地在消防车上爬上爬下。他穿上了消防队员的制服、靴子和帽子,当然,是最小号的。杰米坐在消防车上,穿着制服,捷克给杰米拍照。

"我能做作一名消防队员吗?"杰米问消防队长。

"当然了!"消防队长说,"等你长大了。"

突然,警报响了。

所有的消防队员跳上消防车,消防车开出消防站。

"Wait!" Jack ran towards the fire trucks, but nobody heard him.

Jamie was riding on the fire truck with other firefighters. He was very excited, and said to himself, "Now I really can experience how a firefighter saves people's lives."

The other firefighters were very concentrated. None of them noticed Jamie.

The fire trucks arrived at a burning house. The whole house was on fire. Two kids were crying with their mother outside the house.

The firefighters started to spray water into the house.

The firefighter chief asked the mom and the kids, "Has everyone come out?"

"Our puppy is still inside. We do not know which room he is in. Save his life, please!" The two boys were still crying.

"We will do our best!" the chief said.

Two firefighters came out of the house and said, "We searched everywhere but couldn't find the puppy."

Jamie moved his nose to sniff. He smelled the puppy. Jamie could not help rushing into the house, because he was still wearing the firefighter uniform.

It was burning inside. There was fire and smoke everywhere. However, with his mouse

杰米传奇（第二卷）

当捷克按下相机快门按钮时，他发现杰米不在照片里。

"等等！"捷克跑出消防站来追消防车，但没有人听到他的话。

杰米与其他消防队员一起乘坐飞奔的消防车。他非常兴奋，对自己说，"我现在真的可以体验消防队员如何救人的生命了。"

其他消防队员精神非常集中。他们没有注意到杰米。

消防车赶到在燃烧的房子。整个房子都在着火。两个孩子与他们的妈妈在房子前哭。

消防队员始向房子喷水。

消防队长问妈妈和孩子："每个人都出来了吗？"

"我们的小狗还在里面。我们不知道在哪个房间，请救救它！拜托啦！"两个孩子还在哭。

"我们将竭尽所能！"消防队长说。

两名消防队员从房子出来，张着他们的双手，说："我们到处搜寻，但找不到小狗。"

nose, Jamie could still follow the puppy smell. He ran through the fire while praying to God. Finally, he found the puppy sleeping on its bed. Jamie picked up the puppy and rushed out of the house.

As soon as Jamie came out of the house, the house collapsed.

People applauded, "You are our hero!" "Brave little mouse!"

杰米传奇（第二卷）

杰米用他的鼻子嗅。他闻到小狗的气味。杰米忍不住冲进了房子。别忘了，他穿着消防队员制服。

里面到处在燃烧。到处是火和烟。然而，凭着他的老鼠鼻子，杰米仍能循着小狗的气味。他穿过火，同时向上帝祈祷。最后，他发现小狗睡在床上。杰米用胳膊抱起小狗，冲出了房子。

杰米刚一出房子，房子就塌了。

人们鼓掌欢呼："你是我们的英雄！""勇敢的小老鼠。"

一句话进到杰米心中，"捷克说：但以理的朋友投入火中去荣耀神。"

他安静地把小狗递给两个孩子。他们非常高兴和感激，他们亲吻了杰米的脸颊。

"说 Je—sus，世界上最勇敢的老鼠。"捷克刚刚抵达,给杰米拍图片。莎莉和安德烈也和他一起到达。

"我们都为你感到骄傲，杰米。"莎莉说。

Some words came into his mind, "Jack said that Daniel's friends went into the fire to glorify God."

He handed the puppy to the two kids. They were so happy and thankful that they kissed Jamie on his cheeks.

"Say 'Je---sus', the bravest mouse in the world," Jack just arrived and took a picture for Jamie. Sally and Andrew also came with him.

"We are proud of you, Jamie," Sally said.

"This action is brave and valuable," Andrew said.

"Thank God I came out safely," said Jamie. "I prayed when I was in the house. I just did what a mouse should do. My whiskers were not burned this time."

"Thank you, brave little mouse. You are already a great firefighter," the chief said, and hugged him.

"这个行动太勇敢，太有价值啦！"安德烈说。

"感谢上帝，我安全地出了房子。"杰米说，"当我在房子里的时候，我不停地在祈祷。我只是做了一只老鼠应该做的。这次，我的胡子没被烧掉啦。"

"谢谢你，勇敢的小老鼠。您已经是一个伟大的消防队员啦。"消防队长说着拥抱他。

Discussion Questions and Activities:

1. Please read Chapter 3 of the *Book of Daniel*. Why didn't Daniel's three friends die in the fire? Are they big heroes?
2. Why did Jamie want to go into the fire? Is it good for Jamie to run into the fireplace?
3. Why did Jamie disappear in Jack's camera?
4. Did Jamie finally become a big hero?
5. Please visit the fire station in your town with your parents.
6. Memorize 1 Corinthians 13:3 "If I give away all I have, and if I deliver up my body to be burned, but have not love, I gain nothing."

杰米传奇（第二卷）

讨论问题和活动：

1. 请阅读《但以理书》3章。为什么但以理的三个朋友没有死在火里？他们是大英雄吗？
2. 杰米为什么要跑进壁炉？这是一个好行为还是一个鲁莽的行为？
3. 为什么杰米在捷克的照相机里消失了？
4. 杰米最后没有成为一个大英雄？
5. 请与父母一起参观镇上的消防站。
6. 请背诵经文《哥林多前书》13:3 "我若将所有的赒济穷人，又舍己身叫人焚烧，却没有爱，仍然与我无益。"

Thank you for reading our stories.
See you soon !

谢谢您阅读我们的故事。
很快会再见哦！

Silly, Silly Mouse
Jamie Book 3
is around the corner !

杰米传奇 （第三卷）
也快出版啦！

It will be available on
www.amazon.com

www.ingramcontent.com/pod-product-compliance
Lightning Source LLC
Chambersburg PA
CBHW031443040426
42444CB00007B/947